Birds And Other Beasts

RICHARD H. PEAKE

Author's Tranquility Press
MARIETTA, GEORGIA

Richard H. Peake/Author's Tranquility Press
2706 Station Club Drive SW
Marietta, GA 30060
www.authorstranquilitypress.com

Ordering Information:
Quantity sales. Special discounts are available on quantity purchases by corporations, associations, and others. For details, contact the "Special Sales Department" at the address above.

Birds and Other Beasts/Richard H. Peake
Hardback: 978-1-958554-36-4
Paperback: 978-1-958554-32-6
eBook: 978-1-958554-33-3

Contents

Acknowledgments

Cumberland, Georgia Review, Impetus,
Jimsonweed, Snowy Egret,
University of Virginia Magazine,
Vision Books, Wind

Dedication

To Catherine Mahony and John Mack Clarke,
who have encouraged me in my writing,
and Martha, my wife, who sustained me

"Some shape of beauty moves away the pall
From our dark spirits" John Keats

"Men are held here
Within a mighty tide swept

onward toward a final sea"

James Still

"No living man will see again the virgin giant

hardwoods"
Aldo Leopold

Preface

My serious attempts to write poetry began when I was an undergraduate at the University of Virginia. A collection of my early poetry was awarded the Mary Cummings Eudy poetry award by the English faculty and led to my becoming the poetry editor of *The University of Virginia Magazine*. As a young faculty member at Clemson University, I was fortunate to place some poems in Impetus together with Hollis Summers and John Ciardi. Some of my early poems such as *Greek Gifts; Malt, Milton, and Mary Jane; A Substitution; Inebriate; Cottonwoods; and Peregrine* appear here without much change. Others have been worked and reworked. Over the years I have continued to write other poetry. *East Beach Birdwalk and Ben Ezra's Fraud.*

More than a decade ago John Mack Clarke persuaded me to allow Vision Books to publish some of my poems under the title of *Wings Across* A few years later he published some more of my poems in a chapbook entitled *Poems for Terence*. I am indebted to John for insisting that I publish my poems, the majority of them for the first time, although a number of them had appeared in journals. Since the publication of the book and chapbook by Vision Books, I have made little effort to publish further poetry, although I have read some of the unpublished poems from time to time. Through the years I have received support and encouragement from Catherine and Jack Mahony, who have read some of these poems in manuscript. Many of these poems—especially sections of *The Door to Door Show and Birding for the Bard*—were well received at my public readings, and I was encouraged to publish them. Excerpts from these have appeared in *Jimsonweed.* As people have expressed a wish to experience *The Door to Door Show* in its entirety, this long poem recently has appeared for the first time in Jimsonweed. I hope this volume will gain a wider audience for this poem and the other poems presented here.

Included in this volume are the poems from my previous volumes of poetry as well as the introduction to *Wings Across* ... written by John Lang, whose critical judgments of that volume I accept without reservation. His comments can be applied to many of the other poems in this volume as well, I believe, although some of these poems place more emphasis upon human nature than do the poems that Lang assessed.

Nevertheless, I do not think that there could be a better introduction to my poetry than Lang's.

To paraphrase Keats, the beauty of imagery drawn from the natural world has always prompted me to wish to drink deeply from the spring of life. I hope these poems prompt readers to see themselves as part of a web of life that startles us with its complexity but offers us a sense of being part of a journey through universal order. Though *Birding the Rio Grande, The Door to Door Show, and Birding for the Bard* are all long poems using the journey motif that organizes *Hiking Down Straight Fork*, the first two of these poems use a loose blank verse rather than free verse, and the third intersperses some free verse within loose blank verse. *The Door to Door Show* was my first long poem developed in loose blank verse stanzas using the journey motif. It and those that followed owe a great deal to the example of Robert Lowell's later poetry, which I studied in depth during a seminar at Rice University with Monroe Spears in 1978. It was during this seminar that I composed the main portion of *Birding the Rio Grande*, which I completed the following year.

—Richard Peake

Shapes of Beauty: Richard Peake's *Wings Across ...*

This first volume of poems by long-time Southwest Virginia resident Richard Peake provides cause for celebration. In its careful, loving attention to the natural world, *Wings Across ...* follows the advice given over a century and a half ago by Ralph Waldo Emerson in his famous essay *Nature*: "wise men ... fasten words again to visible things." This Richard Peake does, participating in a long tradition of American nature poetry that began with Anne Bradstreet's *Contemplations* and continues in our own day.

An amateur ornithologist and experienced bird watcher, Peake revels in what fellow poet Jeff Daniel Marion has called the "miracles of the air." Birds appear in poem after poem in this collection, most notably in the book's longest single work, *Birding the Rio Grande*, a five-part poem some twenty pages in length. Across these pages soar Bewick's wrens, Botteri's sparrows, brown jays, paraques, golden -cheeked warblers, chachalacas, and a myriad of other birds. But *Birding the Rio Grande* does not simply catalogue their existence; it also explores humanity's relationship to nature and the poet's relationships to his father and his son, the latter of whom accompanies the poet on this journey of discovery. The poem gains depth by using the archetypal journey motif and by drawing upon humanity's ancient fascination with flight. Moreover, the natural world the poet portrays is both beautiful and fragile, both resilient and vulnerable.

The splendor of oleander hides oil tanks and U-Totem stores, and cliff swallows have learned to nest under bridges. Yet "sugar cane and concrete/ have eaten huisache bushes and mesquite." Like Robert Frost in *The Oven Bird*, Peake often sees about him "diminished things." His poems must arise, in large part, out of the desire to preserve and to praise nature's endangered beauty. His song, like that of the oriole he hears, incorporates "the sum of a world's scattered forms saved." It is "an anthem against ... forgetfulness."

From this journey south, the poet and his son return with minds and spirits refreshed, with "wings across our thoughts," the phrase that gives this book its title. Immersion in nature nourishes the human imagination, for "vireos feed our minds as they feed flesh," the poet writes. The experiences this poem recounts, in its loose blank verse lines, aid the reader's recovery of nature as a resource and instill a right regard for human limitations, a healthy humility in the presence of a world we did not and cannot make. The poem's closing line mirrors the contrast between the human and the avian realms both thematically and structurally, with its two initial trochees in an otherwise iambic line: "Heavy, earthbound, men soar as best they can."

Natural objects and features of nature predominate in the other four sections of *Wings Across*...as well. The opening section, for instance, entitled *Hiking Down Straight Fork*, recalls A. R. Ammons' dictum that "A Poem is a Walk." Here, as in *Birding the Rio Grande*, Peake focuses on water as a fundamental natural element, essential to sustaining life. Four of the poem's six parts take their titles from the names of branches flowing into Straight Fork. Like many Southern writers, Peake expresses a love of place, especially of natural landscapes, that is complemented by a sense of history, both human and natural. *Hiking Down Straight Fork* beneath "a sky as blue as Wedgewood," the poet observes a soaring red-tailed hawk and notes that the same species floated above generations of Cherokee and, more recently, above lumbermen and coal-company surveyors. Though his eye is that of the naturalist, this poet is always conscious of the region's human his-tory as well. Amidst the bulldozer's "spoor of spoil" darkening the fork, he urges his readers to recall and respect nature's grandeur.

Yet Peake's attitude toward nature, it should be emphasized, is not that of the sentimentalist. Section II of *Wings Across ...* consists of three poems grouped under the general title *Wild Things*. Whereas Emerson heard nature thundering the Ten Commandments, Peake presents the reader, in *Winter Fare*, with a Darwinian struggle for survival, one creature feeding another "as form gives way to form." For all its Edenic qualities, nature's order is built on blood. Preying—not praying— is its vital principle, as is also evident in the poems *Peregrine, Harlequins*, and *Impassive Gazer*. The last of these, a poem reminiscent of Emerson's *Brahma*, invokes the Hindu god Shiva, who "feed[s] the roots of changing form." For Peake, however, the destruction evident in nature is part of a larger creative process that breeds life, just as Shiva is the god not only of destruction but of reproduction. Thus, even such dark poems as *Peregrine and Harlequins* occur in the section of

Wings Across ... entitled *Celebrations.* Similarly, the book's concluding section, Adaptations from the German, traces a seasonal cycle that begins and ends with spring (though summer poems are notably absent, poems of fall and winter predominating instead). In this final section poems such as *Migration Paths and Fall Flight* reinforce the distance between humanity and such natural phenomena as birds. At the same time, through its epigraph from Columbus' diary, *Fall Flight* reminds the reader of nature's diminishment over centuries of human abuse. We in the late twentieth century need to recover the explorer's sense of awe, Peake suggests, and he underscores this idea by raising questions in the poem's second stanza that resemble those posed to Job out of the whirlwind, questions meant to reveal to Job his place in a universe beyond human making.

Although death is inevitable, the poet accepts that fate in nature's design, however impersonal that design may be. In fact, in *Spring Rack,* the book's final poem, Peake envisions himself dead amidst what he calls "the revelry of grave." Instead of lamenting his demise, he welcomes the transformation death brings. Each of the poem's five stanzas ends with a reference to the laurel that grows from his decaying corpse. Here is a poet, then, willing to forgo the traditional laurel wreath as an emblem of poetic achievement for the sake of the living laurel.

Lest anyone assume that Richard Peake is a poet of only one mood or subject or one literary form, I should add that he works skillfully in a variety of modes: loose blank verse, rhymed traditional forms, free verse (occasionally rhymed), and syllabics. In addition to the many poems in which nature is his principal subject, readers will find in this finely crafted volume love poems, meditative poems, portraits of people, and the moving *For Robert Lowell: January, 1978*, one of the book's best. This book abounds in beautiful lines and images: "The black-necked waders cry in their wet fields," for example, and "skies the white-faced ibis soars." Such lines embody, in Fred Chappell's phrase, "the eye's joy."

What Peake says about sighting a rare green kingfisher in *Birding the Rio Grande* can be said as well about the poems themselves: "Delight follows discovery."

—John Lang
Emory & Henry College

Hiking Down Straight Fork

I On the Ridge

Topping the ridge that fronts the Cumberland's
talking dam
talking flood
talking wilderness,
words scurrying the air like chipmunks leap the
leaves and trunks of our advent
as we announce our jumping off on journey.

In the rubbled clear cut the juncos mill
while hikers circle restless for their plunge
down the road
to intersect with Big Oak Branch
where poplar grow tall
in the floodplain
of imagination's sunlight enclave carved
by the men who chopped oak down to size.
Whose size?
Theirs?
Or generations' yet to come?

On a way was a trail before a wagon road
we drove up Powell Mountain from Back Valley
under a sky as blue as Wedgewood china.

Uplifting a hawk the Cherokee named
eagle with the red tail
who hovers high
on thermals holds himself aloft above
a noisy group who sense his majesty
and yell and gape and point their praise
as the autocrat surveys his two square miles
of mice and meals
marking their paths
while our boots stumble by with awkwardness:
Circle upon circle he draws out
ascending—
upward, the sure-winged god
whistles his triumph.

Our collected aspirations move forth
hiking down Straight Fork to Carter's Store.
We follow the road,
the trail,
the railroad bed
and feel the wilderness envelop us
though every step uncovers artifacts
of hunt,
and dig,

and lumbermen who built
their narrow gauge
through the gigantic oak, hickory
maple to render yard-wide boards
from Boone's forest

where the whitetail waved
 its flag at the Shawnee and Cherokee
and settler,
indifferent in aplomb.

II Big Oak Branch

Our hunting group finds the spoor
with quick eyes
that lead us as noses led old *habilis*...

Like a beacon in carefully raked sea
of reddish dirt a scent trap waits to track
the nosy animals that come to smell.

A little farther on, some more debris
in the road—
the white tape marks the spot
for helicopter coal survey that's gone,
but not the tape—
Consol's X marks the spot.
Then jumping off,
crashing down the hillside

into the lean tulip trees sentinel
over giant rhododendron thickets:
hearing the dee-dee-dee of chickadee
we salute *Parus atricapillus*...

Yanked up from the stream salamanders
squirm out of the grasping hand,
duskies
squirm before their caudal appendages
reveal whether they are fuscus or seal.

Along the stream we pick up leaves.
Look up.
What's this, sourwood?
Well, I guess,
how can we tell these leaves?
See there?
Up at the top, up eighty feet,
those leaves shout *Tilia americana!*
Hey, so do these,
these nutlike fruits hanging
on slender stalk from narrow bract of leaf.

O, where is the flowery white of summer
when Swainson's warblers sing the cooling
stream, the stream that laves the trees with
hands of mist
bathes *Dryopteris intermedia,*
bathes *Polystichum acrostichoides*

and encourages moss to cover trunks
of the fallen chestnut, oak, and maple,
covers the trash,
covers the iron,
covers the buckets
left by lumbermen on Big Oak Branch.

III White Rock Branch

On white rocks ravished by the April flood we
sit to eat our lunch.

Look at this rock
 gouged by the force,
wiped clean of algae
for a new beginning
shining white
and pink and blue.
Kaleidoscopic sun
dances across the water
running clear
enough to drink
but fierce to gouge white rock.
Rock movement here too slow for us to feel,
but we can hear the woodpecker tap wood,
see the water crash the stillness of the pool,
and listen to the laughter of the crows
who cry our hike,
yet we pass unrecognized
granitic strength that molds in silence.

IV Church Rock Branch

Just below the Church Rock we stand and wait
at Lane Camp Branch beside the yellow birch
at prayer—
forced to kneel over the Straight Fork
the birches bare their roots torn from the rock,
their tenuous grip concealed in the deep dirt.

Watching eddies in the pool at Lane Camp
where its water hits the force of Straight Fork
clouding the bottom rocks:
silt pushes gray
opaque over the pool in murky forms
as seers read the sign of the bulldozer
hidden from their view.

The spoor of spoil flows
thick,
casting its dirt on Straight Fork's clarity.

Through the rhododendron of Church Rock
Branch we tread,
white water below and hemlock
along a trail that sometimes humps the hill
for slumping down the slope toward the stream
like an avalanche of trees and black spoil.

Rounding a bend,
we look over the hollow

and see an ochre wall rising sheer
above a bare bench undecorated
by yellow machines rusting in the sun:
further on
we find fifty-foot oaks
thrown into Straight Fork from the bench above.
Across the swift water of Straight Fork
a forest lingers cool and dark with hemlock.

V Devil's Fork

As we draw closer to the Devil's Fork
we see a rock face sheltering the bank,
climb the slope to stand under rocky roof
where John "Cliff " Kerns raised a big family,
digging coal and hauling it down the stream
to Ft. Blackmore.
Scratching among the rocks
we turn up the top of John's coal stove
and soles of what must have been his wife's
shoes.

We scratch at John's bones as he scratched at
bones of psilophytes or grubbed up market
roots.
He dug blackberry,
cohosh black or blue,
squirrel corn, mandrake, and
most prized of all,

Sang, ginseng, *Panax quinquefolium*, Chinese folk
food to give fertility.
John dug these roots to sell at Ft. Blackmore,
but used the sassafras himself for tea
and gathered dock and dandelion or mustard
greens and cress to mix with tender poke
so his wife could set a mess of salat greens.

Like the ravens nesting on the cliffs
above the Devil's Fork,
Cliff Kerns came black
from his coal shaft where he crawled a long day
and chipped at the black face
of the bare coal seam
and loaded nuggets he grubbed
into a pony cart.

VI Water Gap

Down to clapboard house deserted now
we hike the final miles of Straight Fork
and settle down to rest
in the seeding grass.

Sitting under apple trees studying the gap
we fight with yellow jackets for the cider
of last fruits
scattered on the ground and limbs.

While the cardinals call we sit and face
the hills
covered with Shawnee war paint.
After a few farewells we climb in cars
to move apart
from Kerns
and Benjy
and Boone
remembering the leafy path down Straight Fork.

Celebrations

For Robert Lowell: January 1978

Here the jackhammer jabs into the ocean

Though you are gone and I years older now
the wind and wave still burst upon black rocks
of the New England coast. They reappear
to those who come to hear the jackhammer sea
or gaze at the gaggle of geese and gulls
and ducks that swim in the winter surf.

O executor of oceanic blues,
you blast and rage against the fluid line
of eternal beach covered with flotsam
that lures the white gull lifted by the air.

Can you feel his fast heart and narrowed wings?
Black rocks remain at Biddeford Pool
to bear the wind and wave that roar the gulf
below the gull that floats the westward breeze.

Greek Gifts

Carry me lightly, carry my bed
across the threshold
into the garden, out to the hyacinths
blooming red and cold
upon the white stone lilies of the dead.

If I must speak, if I must talk
about the world's end
I will not, I cannot offers
hollow gifts to send
to bodies withered on their stalks.

offers up a flower, offers a rose
with a thorn or two
for the all-knowing gardener
who plants the bulbs, who wipes the dew away
with the spout of his hose.

Residue

Sheen of fireflies
seen in loose flight
flaming through the dusk,
without the bugs to fire them
the vegetables and flower plants
fade away.
With them comes a sound
in an eager ear

and a throb in the chest
singing in the key of desire.
Upon this newly shaken star,
our world,
the days and nights breathe
beauty flashing light
in the evening.

Darkness follows, then morning
that sharpens with an iron file
the dull knife of longing
for soft and warm embracing skin
velvet for flight down a scented aisle
toward a key above
the gale ringing
the grinding voice of love.

Love sounded in salt cinders and mist
molders among shadows
on lips of remembrance that insist
of roamed over thighs and of fallow
lust gentling as a face bends its wind
down on another's field to blend.

A wish runs by the mind
like a brushfire
turning reason to black
smoking ash.
A pile of dust remains

and chemical analysis
reveals much calcium
and many traces of elements
the rains will turn to lettuce and mint
and coreopsis and chrysanthemum
to delight the bugs
and light the fire.

Sails from the Orient

"Those were the times," the old lady said,
"when the white-rigged ships brought incense
from Cathay to waft me a delicate murmur
of golden, silent faces politely eating mince
and sipping their unlemon-puckered tea."

"Don't mind her," said Joseph, and reached
me another, more modern social drink;
though I, polite to memory, muttered a demur
before I lifted up the proffered glass.

"The birds came every spring then,"
she told us as she continued tatting,
"I liked to think how neat they had returned
from the other hemisphere, but I knew
the summer's heat would make them somber."
"Get her," Joseph whispered with superior wit,
"the old girl has a feather fetish;

doesn't she know she banked her fire forty years
ago?
Besides, she's lived with steamboats all her life,
and they don't give a damn for sailed exteriors."
She droned on about the beatific birds
of spring that had disappeared down the
horizons of those far-of festival summers
when she had bewitched men instead of thread,
about the numerous wedding cakes her mother
baked,
too late, and how the bird nests
used to tumble down the chimney before Joseph
put detestable central heating in the hall and
ended dreams of sailing ships.

Inebriate

Two soft doves on straight wings over a bush of
red quince are my love's eyes
that sit soft and pliant
above the wet shawl of her lips.

Sweet fresh apples on a high branch
under the windy dress of the sky
are my love's breasts
that quickly rise and fall
in the veined white of her skin:
and I would share the flight
and taste the sweetness of the fruit.

Two white birches side by side
bending across a dark mountain
are my love's arms
tapering from firm shoulders
over the shadow of her hair.

Warm, summer hills
rippling in a soft breeze
are my love's legs
glistening in deep twilight
before the red wine of her thighs:
and I would bend the birches
and dream upon the hills.

Taps

A wood pewee
whistles and mourns
in dusty dark.

I stare at empty sky
and listen to crickets drone—
do you wait in dusk?

At my foot a leaf moves,
red as blood that flows
from a cut on my hand—

red as blood that burns
when my dark reverie
remembers your touch.

Panther Knob

Solstice sun burns
at the painter's throat
melting its white.
At rest in a bough
of the reclining cat
a rusty blackbird
whistles kee-o-lee
from the leafless tree
over the dark back
after winter sun
in somber decline
lets the wind chill
the painter's hide.

Reverie

I am alone at midnight.
The rabbits shiver
under the snow banks,
and under the blanket
my arms ache
for the lover
whose face I cannot see.
Her hand caresses me

in dream.

Gray horses
charge on a field of cloud,
race the winds,
swift across paddocks
of salt-marsh grass,
past the pole at the far turn
of Bodie Island light,
past the slender form
thrust up from the sand.

The gallop of red stallions
careens across the clouds
formed by warming sun
to cool the beach
on which the Atlantic
throws kiss upon kiss.
I lie on the shimmering sand without a
footprint—the sun embraces me.
The breeze tingles.
With a lover's touch
it teases emptiness.
As the gulls laugh
a brown arm blocks the sun
and arches over my head.

Bright eyes unwrap me,
their warmth

like the sun.

The screams of the gulls
echo in my mind
like voices in a dark hall.
I wander the wax myrtle maze
behind the dunes
and scavenge wood
to match my horses.

Then blue horses race
The evening sun to rest—
sea moods shift
like the geese of snow
that straggle skeins in the light.
I pluck out their down
in setting sun
and ride
on white wings.
A lover's hand
 offers me a drink
from a crystal goblet
filled with wine
drawn from fountains of spice.
Her voice on the April wind
whispers my name—
only she can hear
my dream.

Light-dark Experiment

Assembled beside a pond
they break out meter sticks
to measure the biomass:
light uncovers

emerald wing
of a brown bird,

flung against
lazuli sky,

in plummeting earthward for a walk
ungainly with the grazing geese
beyond the gaze of workers
spreading bottles on the waters

finding life
in the pond
dark with algae.

Leaping fish announce
tingling ears immeasurable waves
on mists of ochre smoke and rock
uncovering grunting caterpillars—
hurling

the green-winged teal
beyond the field.

Peregrine

in gunpowder sky

aglow with sunset,

a mourning dove in straight flight
over a field of brush
where I stand hidden
watching swift movement

suddenly

broken

by the strike of talons

downtoppling on bowbent wings

stooping

on the soft feathers—
bird with the black mask

STRIKES!

(lover striding fire and feeling of spherical bust)

rowing wings
leap forth a falcon force ascending,

guy talons trailing blood.

Warlord of the upper air.

Impassive Gazer

Lone Shiva is the stony god
who contemplates both birth and death,
the change from foetus to the clod uniting earth
again with earth.

When sky blends wind and sun with bird
Shiva is the master there;
when talons topple down unheard
the falcon launches Shiva's spear.

Shiva fills the egg and womb,
watches doves and rabbits born
before he sees them to the tomb
to feed the roots of changing form.

Shiva watches hawk and hare,
the falcon and the fleeing dove;
his wraithlike gaze is clear and bare
of sentiment for strife he wove.

Virginia Razorbill: Museum No. 4021

A drowned Alcidian sailor
lies before us on the beach
half-covered by the winter sand. Reverently we
lift the body high

who stand awe-struck to find it there,
saddened that his fishing days
have ended: swimming on the waves
this beauty would have brought us joy.

Picked up from the sand, a razorbill
reveals unhappy death in youth
by his dark and half-grown beak.
That bill will cause fish no fear.

The harsh wind from the bay
little comforts us who mourn a bird
whose strangeness to this shore
dictates it lie in state as specimen.

Feathery suit of formal black
and white must grace a museum case
and gain a numbered immortality
far from the ice floes of his youth.

Flocks of scoter blacken sky above the bay
and the large gulls hover,
scavengers angrily mourning lost corpse
as they wheel above us.

Transition

Swifts stutter in autumn air,
chitter and sift insects in the gray light,
whirling through the half-knitting sky
into October chimneys.
Autumn is for apple trees
and the last bee workers
in labor on the goldenrod
of a roadside close to the riverbed
and to the season where gray clouds
hitch-hike on an asphalt sky,

bound far and high
on cold thumbs to catch a ride
with the files of geese
winging, winging, winging
in forks from the Back Bay
to the corn-stubble in the fields.

Harlequins

Caracaras
laughing at noon
bash meat of a coon

to blue flesh barrows,
tasty carrion
for Caracaras—
clownish waste barons
live on dead flesh
moved by worm harrows
dressing meat fresh
for Caracaras,
who laugh at sun's baste
warming bone marrows
to epicure taste
of Caracaras.

Cottonwoods

The willows of the desert
are the cottonwoods
who sit tall
and lean
along the stream in council
about
the asphalt of the motor road
that moves
sinuously
where buffalo stood
on the grass that fed Indian ponies.
Until
the long rifle spoke
with a finality

in the sunrise
as
the mountain man sought food.

But the cottonwood
does not seem to be
a tree
with weeping tendency,
and even if it were,
its tears
would get
short-shrift
from a dried-up stream bed
lying inimical
under
the desert sun
watching gila monsters
on the ground
and buzzards in the air.

Final Solution

Roan monkeys spout in wrath
 to ancient Hindus
left in Borneo holes
with bright but dusty wraiths.

Leopards growl and dart
at jungle redwings

of Angkor black in ruin,
great, majestic, and deaf.

Gazelles run the Khan's gain
of sands to Samarkand
from the empire of Kin
while spears rust to grit.

Afghans have found their graves
on cold Himalayas;
no Afghan kings on horse
raise their swords from the ground.

Binoculated Snipe

The stolid, humble tiller of the land
stands by his fence and smokes a pipe
in silent wonderment about the band of stalkers
who binoculate his snipe.

Fearlessly they tramp his marshy bogs
chasing cows and chickens everywhere.
Without a thought of omnipresent hogs,
they stop knee deep in muck to stare.

"What are you looking at?" the farmer asks,
and shakes his head when they reply, "Your
snipe."

While all the watchers reassume their masks,
the farmer looks amused and puffs his pipe.

Sky Tracks

Whorling up, a snowy mass churns
its ink-tipped arching feathered wings
above the darkened stubble in the burn
men charred for greener marsh when spring
comes grassy mantle cracking blackened earth
while white birds beat on overhead the bay,
their color hiding wrack
they rend in winter fabric's spread
as snow geese rise to wing *en masse*
north to their tundra home once more.
Flight brings flight as birds move past
on aero tracks their ancestors wore.

Capital Snowbirds

Gallows drew a man from earth inert
jerking rope of toughest hemp
iron shod with flecks of frozen dirt:
silhouette whose collar held him limp
under the white ptarmigan, dangling hurt—
bird's flight defying puppet's eyes
whose jellied gaze seemed wise.

Lifeless eyes stared at winter air
after wheat preening golden pods

under summer's cloudy brood mares
sweating dirt into greening sod.

A corpse was roughly put to bed.
They who dropped him there have trod
the rocky ground that Judas fled.

Quick hand slash threw one thought stranger
hanging dead down onto frozen grime.
He seemed harbinger of danger,
not their brotherhood in crime.
Sanguineless was put to bed betimes
a man whose fellows watched him swing
and heard the white snow crunching.

Bound by hat Music

Many youths caught in love's harsh music
remind me of that Nashville Warbler
we found on a foray in Virginia
among the northern hardwoods and spruce
and a lone tamarack where he picked a bog
he liked and set up shop to sing his song.
He didn't seem to mind that we who heard
thought him an oddity who wouldn't find
a mate. He had the confidence of youth,
for he was sounding still his ringing call
when we forsook our wilderness he owned.

Were those emphatic calls we stalked to hear
wasted? Certainly they were not meant for us
though we happened by to notice them
and reacted with a fervor kin to his
to find him so far south of normal range.
I hail youths' rock rhythms. They hurt my ears,
yet the primal urge brings all songs to birth.

Litmus Flight

A white-winged gull invaded my youth
on a spike of light from the cold, gray truth
of an April day. I braced against the gale
blowing from the east as I stood with my back
to the tidal flats along the river's track.

Against the April sky my litmus gull
turned pink to raise the ph of my soul.
Whipped by the gusting wind, it soared and told
its rippling wings to stride the roller coaster air.
I wracked my brain to try to join it there,

but my bright gull ascended into clouds
still crying its strength and grace so proudly
that my feet grew heavy with weight of man
as they sank into the river mud and sand,
earthbound, not fit to pass the acid test.

Harsh Gossamer: Netting Birds

In the afternoon I walk softly
Down the hollow and drop in place my nets
To catch unwary birds that hit the web
I've set to capture curious flight.
The tufted titmouse screams as my hand frees
Its wing. Somewhere deep within me cries
A captive answering the caught bird's desire
For feathers striding wind to fly away.
After I take them from my nylon web
I carefully place a band upon one leg.

Then I measure the bird, and let it go.
Other netters net for meat, not science.
Like giant spiders that set delicate nets
To gain a feathered meal, these netters place
Homemade webs along the paths where birds fly
Moving north or south as nature dictates.
All spider, they spread their nets for food.
They quickly eat the birds they catch, relish
the savory meat of avian breasts
without a twinge of guilt or pity.

Sumo

On the smooth, wet sand
shorebirds spatter by us like corks,

bobbing heads and running in bursts at the land,
splashing stranded water, saluting the sharks
who play beyond their surfing band.

Awestruck, on the shifting dunes
we keep time with beat of the surf
welcoming the cloud-wandering moon
to the wrestling match below the turf
of dune grass. We share the view with grebes
and loons.

Flexing its muscular hide
the ocean churns up white caps
and coughs out the rinds of ships that defied
its strength. Watching waves from the shore
they slap we sense the thundering waters' stride.

Prelude to Flight

Avian eyes peer through the trees
standing under their airy road
as the breeze
strikes red and yellow birds to goad
them, urging flight to stroke
the skies above the oaks.
Their wings rift
air in a frenetic, twittering surge
as their urge lifts
them up and feathers merge

with the moonlit heights
of their long night.

Neotropic Migrant

Every spring an April fool
Announces the snow's defeat
And claims its fast retreat
Will let the rule
Of bees return upon the clover,
Winter's over.
Then orchid flowers
Shoot up under the cleats
Of vernal showers
And the sun's hot feet.
Defying a late freeze
In budding trees
A red-eyed bird
Makes himself heard.
That emphatic bird
Incessantly sings
And makes tree trunks ring
Even in mid-day heating
Until the summer's over—
Says that summer's end never
Comes while a vireo's heard,
But early frosts deny bird's
Incessant cries for summer.

Galveston Beach Birdwalk

On the right we have a Caspian Tern.
Don't confuse it with the Royal nearby.
They're both big birds and new birders yearn
to turn them into Sandwiches. Who knows why.
No, Mary, I don't mean the kind you eat.
I mean the Sandwich Tern. It's smaller
and has a yellow tip to its bill, I repeat,
It's not a gull or heron. They're taller.
Look at that gray and reddish bird out there
running madly around with wings outstretched.
That's a Reddish Egret. There are a pair
of those running clowns. Look! They're catching
fish by spreading out their wings to get
their prey—a sight you won't soon forget.

See those black-backed birds with orange bills
that seem to flush without provocation.
Watching them when they skim the water thrills
anybody whose soul's not on vacation.
The long lower mandible seeks out fish
as skimmers fly in careful formation
hunting with technique we think outlandish,
yet we look in wonder at their action.
It awes us to see their numbers beat air
wheeling back and forth as if on some cue
eluding us. We cannot fathom where

that Peregrine that launched this melee flew.
The hunter stooped on skimmers bringing shock
to end the noontime siesta of the flock.

There, on sand, a Piping Plover scurries
in straight line. Suddenly she stops and throws
her head back, as if she's greatly displeased
with what's ahead, as if a plover knows
it doesn't pay to move too fast and miss
a worm or other prey. Her behavior
separates her from sandpipers on this
beach, scuttling back and forth seeking favors
washed from the Gulf. Plovers and sandpipers
must contend with man and the dog he brings.
These foes harass less than developers
whose machines destroy dunes and flush wings
to places less fraught with man's intrusions,
but birds don't mind our scoping them for fun.

Hey! To your left are large shorebirds, Mary.
They wear tuxedoes and long, thick red bills
that open oysters with no shucking fee.
Oystercatchers roam oyster bars to fill
their stomachs with tasty delicacies.
It's plain their bills are utilitarian
but beautiful. Like the yellow beaks
on those Great Egrets fishing there, they can
kill. Down the beach you should see pelicans—
notice that the white ones are a third again

larger than the browns: two species whose plan
for fishing is quite different. The brown's plain
force. See that dive. The whites swim in a group.
In a circle, they herd fish in, then scoop.

Look there. Those Neotropic Cormorants
stay here throughout the year unless winter's
weather gets too harsh. These birds need no
plants, only fish to warm their belly feathers.
Double-crested Cormorants come down south
for winter. Larger, they like the ferry
landing, rougher waters, and the bay's mouth.
You tell the two apart by their throaty
patches. It's yellow on the bigger bird
and angles down straight at ninety degrees
while the Neotropic's throat looks blacker.
But either's beak can give the fish a squeeze.
Our East Beach walk won't be complete today
until we see these shags find fish to slay.

No Redbreast Herald

I saw a robin the other day. It bled
in a winter field whose sky was cold,
and geese and snow stood overhead.
I'm not like those ladies who are told
to phone the papers every spring
to tell about the robin hopping
and pulling worms on Sally's lawn.

My robins aren't absolved from ice,
they're my companions of every dawn.
Come down into a swamp woods right
below a pine-scrubbed Virginia hill
when the water's high on the tupelo
and covers the cypress knobs until
you see what I said you could. You go
see a robin chucking in a holly bush
and blackbirds sounding a rusty hinge
as sun shines down in a sudden rush
when the gray and thickened clouds impinge
on squirrels chattering about nuts crushed
to brave cold metaphor with tasty heat
for melting figures wrapped against the sleet.

Our Lady of the Hawks

There are those in our society who scoff
At chasing birds without rifle or shotgun
They laugh at binoculated scoping toffs
Who think a terrific look gives lots of fun,
That added to their lists a rare wildfowl
Is better fare than roasted ptarmigans.
Whether we wanted a hawk or owl
Myriam Moore helped us to praise and prowl.
She knew the way to make birds seem *chic*
To folk who heretofore deemed it antique
Or quaint to rise at dawn to count a rail
And search in fields' odd hours for a quail.

We'll miss her when the hawks are flying
through,
But in her honor we must count a few.

Snowy Owl in Virginia

My joy depended
on a misplaced waif
whose advent ended
my long wait.

There he sat before flight
in the mouse-rich field,
a huge mass of white
whose fate was sealed.

Followed, haunted, gazed
at by hordes of people—
his yellow eyes looked dazed,
the pupils widely dull.

He did not eat the voles
and rats that he could see.
He longed for the cold
and starved amid plenty.

Not yet dead, examined carefully,
a rare bird for my tally.
Ave atque vale.

Trapping Light

The bright world around shouts color to us,
but we see rainbows with distorted lens,
both fleshy lenses nature gives for focus
and tools on which our photo forms depend.

The play of light upon our world betrays the
magic way feathers can trap sunbeams,
but tensile strength of feathers makes strange
plays: what's dull can sparkle evanescent gleams

when the sun's rays strike our large eye's
delight, but then the sun shifts and a bird turns
gray—
its electric blue transformed without the light.
Refracted light creates a bright display

when myriad feathers trap the sun's rays—
a nonpareil bursts in bright flame anew.
What seemed a burned out coal just yesterday
becomes an indigo bunting—bright blue.

A company of eye, and sun, and stance
determine how we move in optic dance.

Death, How Can You Be Proud?

Soaring buzzards flash a sign of death
that should remind us of Prometheus,

yet for years men have learned the shibboleth
that humbleness gives us impetus to heaven.
So we all have kept our livers
from the feasts of vultures and from Lucifer.
For as long as man has known that death
finds all us men, followed by great buzzards,
we poor mortals have cursed and spent our
breath on our hatred of night's darkness and the
guard we all must keep against defiant end.
We find a carcass round and ripe too morbid
and must approve the nausea that contends
against our thinking buzzards intrepid.

We see buzzards soaring and sailing, their wings
dipped with white, a flapping menace obsessive
like the whiteness Ishmael's great whale brings
to spite our Ahab, silence expressive
of grim origins that make us doubt that white
things will live as did the Phoenix —we dislike
to see intrinsic virtue in a dog stripped
bare by Jove's gigantic vultures. The decay
of a dog covered in black is a display
as old as the pyramids of Egypt
or the cleaners perched upon the Parsees'
ground.
We may never accept a death as proud
when it smells of stinking birds and makes a
loud, discordant music on a swelling hound.

Birding the Rio Grande

I On the Road

Prelude to Texas, the swamps of the coast
stretch along the highway in bayou country
while we crane our necks to see the herons
soaring with necks tucked in and legs stretched
out, a stance that looks comic, though efficient
to my son and me, speeding intruders thrusting
over concrete stilts into Eden.

Later, on dry land we water the roadside and
whiff the gas which seeps from loosened pipes
that have ravished the entrails of the earth.

The black-necked waders cry in their wet fields.
The black francolin sings his harlequin *Beep
Boop Beep Boopy Oop* from a tall pine, another
interloper staking a claim.
Searching for the glories of San Jacinto we climb
into our second skin, a shell that sends a sense of
power through our nerves as we, now godlike,

start the car and set a dynamo at hum for the inner man, a sensuous harmony these fields don't bring.

We had this once before, in the first garden just for a moment, but now in chariots we gods can roam our ordered networks that crisscross crazily on the stretching plains of Texas, home of the steer, the lone star and consummate passion of the motor car that carries us easily over the trail the wagons lumbered to the Alamo. Turning south we leap toward the Rio Grande under skies the white-faced ibis soars over roads where scissor- tails catch flies fuming the humid air. Along the sea at Galveston a Gulf breeze burns our cheeks as we eye pelicans from a parking lot. Down the Peninsula we trek the sands now conquered by the crab-like homes on stilts and hurry on to meet the southern night of heat, mosquitoes, and paraque whose plaintive purrweeel is funeral dirge for bugs. It calls us to a midnight pause within our sleeping bags against the ground. Awake, we slap some mosquitoes uncaught by the paraque or the nighthawks.

Clouds dot the sky that stretches horizons, mile after mile of sorghum in the sun except where thin thickets hint that flatness was not always so tame. A roadside stop, planned for breakfast and parula warblers, offers Turk's caps in the shade of oaks where tropical kingbirds yell of danger as we invade, despite the sign: *Watch For Snakes*, though flowers crimson and gold underfoot would tempt us to dream another Eden, if we weren't too busy dodging cow dung and drinking color, to consider serpents.

After we break camp under cloudless sky we move across the plains, and I have time to contemplate the vitality of youth that presses us along his way. The terms are even here. What advantages gray hairs give fade before the heat, the youth, the fare of this new world. A time was, I remember, when I could face eternity that way and didn't hug each morsel of beauty as if it might be my last. I thought romantically of death but didn't know him well enough to see his vacant eye in the return of earth's quick children, the lily, the rose, the sun on marsh at dusk.

Still, the new bird surges through my body—with double exultation I shout out, my son's careful excitement reminds me of my buoyant birds of youth, but I share with him what Father and I shared rarely, a oneness of heart, and mind, and soul— a black-bellied tree duck accomplished that, breaking across the blue, *Dendrocygna autumnalis*, our spring though in my autumn.

His flight in the sun must count for the gamble his parents took that he might give a race to dragons of twentieth-century man. I stand face to face with filial love, whose breath is life, the sharp, the bright, the rough.

II Brownsville

We find Laguna Atascosa, the Gulf again, and the gulf between the old world and the new. The sugar cane and concrete have eaten huisache bushes and mesquite so fast they have developed indigestion: Harlingen, Brownsville, and Port Isabel, where oleanders, red and pink and white, show their splendid hues in front of hovels, oil tanks, highways, and U-Totem stores.

There everyone takes the Yankee dollar from the gringo tourists with a curse, for city men like some kinds of green though they hate mesquite. At noon we stop to hear the chachalacas laugh at us.

In the willows and brush of the refuge the racket of chachalaca sounds outdoes even the comical

rounds of great-tailed grackles, whose cackles'
infinite variety seems subterfuge.
Karrack! Whoever heard of clowns in black?

The lordly great-tail struts his feather stuff upon
the ground before us and his mate, who admires
the shine on his coat and voice, the *savoir-faire*
of Don Giovanni lightening the all-brooding
world she lives. Watching her sidle, we are
caught in the yellow eye of the grackle and
cavort in glee to the tunes he chortles and
cracks.

Myriad small birds leap in sudden flight; they
throw their sparks of red, blue, gold, and green
into an American sky, defying gravity, buntings
painting our heaven, though the old runways
remind us sternly that these acres of brush once
served to train young men for flight into
blossoms of flak in machines groaning,
defecating bombs before the keen-eyed hunters
killed those geese.

At least the splattering excretions dropped by
chachalacas and buntings will fertilize the field
to bring new growth, not flowers more savage
than all the weeds.

What we really seek here, though, are small,
brown little sparrows, found nowhere else with
ease in these United States. Scarcity gives
Botteri's sparrows a bit of class we think, who
brave the mid-day heat to hear them sing.
Otherwise how can we tell them: they look so
much like Cassin's sparrows.

So we drive through the brush along bayside and
listen. One sings, we stop, intently gazing at the
song. A bronzed cowbird hears it too, and flies
to look, his red eye glaring at us and searching
for the singer fled from parasite. Later we find a
song for us, lifted beyond the cowbird's stare.

III Santa Ana

Technology presses against Santa Ana.
Two thousand acres is all that's left
of the brushland that set the Rio Grande
apart from the southern Texas plains—
now farms and factories call a modern dance,
circle left and sugar dough, swing your gal,
then head for easy, air-conditioned home
to match your tractor's radio, cool cab,
and filtered glass that saves you from the glare
of a fervid sun against a humid sky.

Along the roads, the paths of Santa Ana
the native birds and plants hunch up for safety.
no other place to flee, the ebony tree
spreads its old age for us and the oriole
building its pendulous nest. Whatever
is fugitive insists on loveliness.

Looking across our supper at my son,
I see my youth beleaguered by my thrust
into the warmth, the old futility
of our single mother's birthing womb
in which we seek the breath, the blood, the kiss
to meld us one with her fertility.
More practical, my boy breaks out the tent
while I daydream about the fathers' eyes
I see through him. Fathers ... old men with a hoe,
you have come back to me, resurrected
in this youth who works so steadily there,
his mechanical skill containing you both,
my stubborn dad, the other dad I loved,
the best men in their best world possible.

Dad's blacksmith shop and fields of wheat and
corn are far from here, but the diminished things
about me turn my mind to losses felt
more deeply than the loss of Texas plants,
yet linked inseparably. Daddy wouldn't leave
the land. He held it for his son and daughter,
a solid gift he would not break for tax—

were they worth it, those long days from the
chair you fought our pleas to sell and live at
ease?
The last hug, the last tying of our eyes
you knew would never meet again in life,
though I, unwilling to accept our fate,
said goodbye and not farewell in that last clinch.
You kept trees green. What more can a man do?

Bentsen State Park and Santa Ana
hoard a remnant of tropical forest,
a miser's pile of dew glittering green
in a morning sun, a cool retreat at noon,
a tired man's bivouac at the evening wind
that springs from southern Texas ground in
gusts of glee whenever the sun goes down.
We drove into camp at Bentsen on the wings
of this breeze that blew us to orioles:
Altimira and black-headed—hard to find
that bird—but he blew in with us and sang
in the hush when the moving trees were still,
his song the sum of a world's scattered forms
saved, an anthem against peals of forgetfulness.

In the evening quiet the doves call softly,
insistently, mourning diminished day.
We search through the mesquite and oak to find
the white-tipped dove's low-pitched ooo-

whooooo that haunts the trees around us,
echoing despair.
Far away, only the hollow, long-drawn whooooo
reaches ears straining to find the source
of all that woeful beauty, that dirge
following the path of a setting sun.
Found at last, the birds show rufous underwings,
throats and foreheads fronted with white.
The light at rest on their bodies turns roseate.
When we are lost in the dark that follows,
I would give eight hours for that late bloom.
A sense of loss colors the wings of morning
before we seek the birds of Falcon Dam.

As we delay our leave from Bentsen,
a harsher note invades the uncupped ears,
a sound in keeping with the raucous note
of the chachalacas: crowing roosters,
the white-winged doves asking, "Who cooks for
you?" at us, sitting below, eating cereal
cold in the open box of convenience—

our spirits soar a little with the hawk, bay-
winged beautiful that graces our sky, but the
brown cowbird, young interloper fed by a tiny
olive sparrow
blind in love, betrays our snug earthly nest.

IV Falcon Dam

We reach our destination in the heat
and view the Rio Grande from Falcon Dam.
Man's work, high, mighty, this raptor cannot fly
With the supple grace of the peregrine
That races river birds for prey each fall.

Golden woodpeckers dig for grubs in the trees
whose painted buntings sing against concrete.
The view from this man-made mountain catches
winding waters. Shallow, still, they wait
the hand that opens gates, creates the rush
upsurging river over the bare rocks.

Now the watching heron spears with ease
the fish collected handily in pools,
his stony cups for drinking frogs and snakes.
Excitement uncontained now, we bound

down the slope to the river's edge. Low water
means we may catch the green kingfisher's act,
a dive to joy made only in clear pools
where minnows cannot elude his beak.
"What's that so swiftly cutting through the air?"

"That there? A swallow by his graceful flight and
the sheen rippling over his back."

Delight follows discovery. This bird is the
emerald we bird fishers seek. Perched, alert, he
allows us his profile,
all beak, removing our lingering doubts.
Health to the beaked, green head! To the destiny
that brought us, anxious, eager, to his fief.

Joy of the bird—we sail with swallows coasting
the river though we sit on the bank on lookout
for that other jewel
of the Rio Grande, the ringed kingfisher,
whose breast emblazoned with brick red sets
fire to our imagination for high flight
that carries us to Falcon Dam State Park,
where nonpareils sing in the mid-day heat that
sears the brush of the desert birds, the
pyrrhuloxias huddled in the shade, pink, tinkling
echoes of woodland beauty set among the devil's
tongue in yellow bloom. Sound and color tipple
eye and ear asking how this harsh world can
conjure vision up.

After noon we seek out what we are told is the
"hottest" birding spot on this river, the Santa
Margarita Ranch we reach despite directions.
From the King of Spain the Gonzales family
gained this land by grant. Raising our binoculars
we say, "pajaros," as instructed, only to hear,
"Two dollars a person to see the birds." Mike

tells us he has come to visit, to help Grandfather. Summer is a holiday from Houston traffic.

In heat we trek to the riverside to search for the only brown jays to cross from Mexico. We find boys spearing carp. Minute follows minute, hour tedious hour, the boys take up their fish and leave us.

Hot and tired and jayless, we hike to car. "No jays," is the sad report we give to Mike. He whispers in Grandfather's ear, then says we can come back tomorrow on the house, no fee. Their birds don't come with guarantee, Mike jokes—brown jay is Uncle's C. B. handle. Jays have a special place in the life here.

Supper at the campground raises our hopes. The cactus wren, the braggart, yells to us, and a scaled quail sits on a bush and screams like a guinea hen, "Jay-ho, jay-ho," as though a thing infallible were planned. In the shower house, after supper, we take off a week of sweat and dirt under a water head, and look for ticks, tiny specks of brown that can balloon out to raise the temperature higher.

We move into the evening wind gusting camp and hike to find a paraque as a full moon cast its samite lightover prickly pear and hides the danger there. Lights from passing cars disturb our eye adjusted shapes. The wind moves on our minds; the red eyes of paraques glare at us when we turn our flashlights on the birds; red flares fly up and mingle with the stars.

V The Road Back

Next morning brings me a jay and a son who gnashes his teeth at me: he didn't see that great brown jay, big as a hawk, that stole upon us in a flock of cousin green jays, who called him in awhile, not long enough. We sit in the cool shade of the river trees and watch the kingfishers green and red shimmer in the early light rushing up the Rio Grande. A mourning dove circles us who have invaded her brooding life and sit beside her nest. Beneath the sun a hawk rises on the heated air.

Time past for hunting jays, we must head north.
Who can live a week back, to find a brown jay?

Sadly retreating to the upland hills
we hear a verdin fussing, feeding young; the trill
of a black-throated sparrow
rings upon awakened ears: sitting on a branch of
mesquite, the stripe-faced bird eases fate.

Our idyll ended, the Rio Grande fades
to memories, bright but poignant with loss of
red-billed pigeons, rare, maroon in sun streaking
shafts across the water's morning birds that fly
away ... wings across our thoughts.

In the shade of a lookout's hill we survey
the Rio Grande. One last time. Mockingbirds
serenade us, vultures circle our sky.
The light that blears my eyes is not the sun.

We move toward the west along the lake— it
touches our path and wets the desert; at the high
bridges swallows mill the air and line the
thickened wire beside the road;
these man-made cliffs the cliff swallows make
home, their concrete crags beside the waters.

As we roll into the streets of Laredo we find the
ballad loses something in translation to another
century.
Rock doves and house sparrows fly from
sidewalks to hide in the Spanish architecture.
The streets of Laredo lack romance now, we spy
tourists and five-dollar bills— the mind travels
uphill in motorcars.
A hundred miles of Texas plain lies between
Laredo and Antonio, and green grass cutting

across the range. The hill country breaks the
flatland at San Antonio,
and here we stop for one last look at birds
before we travel east. Friedrich Park glows as we
climb up in the evening sun amid the noise of
Bewick's wrens who scold our search through
pine and oak to find golden-cheeked warblers
and black-capped vireos. Rufous-crowned
sparrows gurgle as we watch fledgling vireos
feed in the dying sun. Vireos feed our minds as
they feed flesh.

Before we get into our car, a lark
sparrow throws his twilight song at the dusk. As
we thrust against the dark of the plains toward
the garish glare of Houston,
this prayer for peaceful sleep softens the air of
sunset behind us. As we move east
gaudy scissor-tailed flycatchers glow in the
departing light and bull-bats flit the sky. The
traffic rushes by us—
to unknown destinies. With bright lamps cars
catapult against our dreams of Eden. The birds
of southern Texas settle
to rest on the mesquite in our minds, burned as
our second gasoline, regret.
Soon my son and I must part—our birds fly in
skies with him, on a sleek super jet;

our birds stay here with me, watching the sky,
wondering where their brothers, sisters go and
whether flight will bring them safe again
together. The sparrows of the airport chirp in
tune to the rock dove's banal coo, dismal
surrogates for the birds of sun we saw when we
birded the Rio Grande.
They do their best, their very homely best, these
foreign feathers that are home here now,
creatures of a feathered beauty that shames the
metallic birds we fly to serve our need. Heavy,
earthbound, men soar as best they can.

Adaptations

Spring

Over the river fly
the seagulls tossed by wind. The ducks chatter
and lie still on the riverbank.

No clouds have climbed higher
than these moments in March.
The seagulls reel and cry
of sunlight on the heart.

September Heat

Hot woman, guard your glowing touch. Though
your heat shrivels anxious grass, the corn loves
your red wine and the clutch of grasshoppers
who sing your praise.

The prairie lark that climbs the blue applauds
your sunny, glittering dawns
and morning glories. Purple dews are shouts of
triumph being born.

Your sparkling nights offers cool balm, a liquor
that helps green grass revive. Snails wander
dew-wet evening calm but don't notice the star-
dappled skies.

Your hot laughter hides fear of frost. Your sticky
toad tongue catches flies.

Your salamander heart is crossed
with browning growth and frequent fires.

No Modern

Easier than Oberon
can mount with locusts and larks
over forest and lake
the mole makes lawns dark.

The myth of Oberon
today excites harsh jibes.
His golden horses limp
whenever he drives.

The old god's harness clinks
as he battles wind
whose force chafes
the rocky harbor, my friend.

Apple Harvest

While ladders poke the apple trees and offers
young men to the evening; they stand sky-high
and fondle honey heaven, full of golden mist.

A radiant morning follows bees as sun
ferments— summer vines
trail through blackberry, thorned memory, apple
scent, nut stain, cider, wine.

Time for a girl and a place to cling.
Ground without girls burns.
Lovers push, thrust face to face, hug in the path,
laugh their desire.
Maple leaves smile red decline, draw glance and
lip to lip.
All things that live demand to find warm love
whose wildfire will consume.

The longed-for paradise holds distress, halts our
bodies and seizes grief— consummate summer,
summer we confess has bees that sting from
their concealment.

Snow Music

I hear music in cold fields.
The winter throws the colorful snow
against the sun to create rainbows.

It plays a music I can feel.

The snowflakes tap a few bars
of brightly-colored blizzard—
of icy flowers, shining stars:
roses bloom out of crystals.

Gentle sounds strike the trees,
where snowroses wax and wane
as snowbirds call quiet refrains
that put discord of heart at ease.

Soft Winter Song

The hunter tightens the noose
but the fox gives him the slip;
the cold wind solders the loose
ice shut over eels and carp.

From arctic cold, the thrushes flee.
Their voices fall gentle on snow;
no knife cuts into earth's sleep,
the mole raises no sores.

Larvae become quiet and wise,
hang in wait for April wind;
udders of pregnant sheep rise,
and the goat's beard lengthens.

Child Roland's Dirge

Horns of summer fall silent in acres of death,
cloud after cloud floats into dark
and circling forests grown thin like mourners
who follow a hearse.

Terrified, the brown fields moan the storm that
strips the poplars to white towers and sweeps
across the barren: gray huts of a village huddled
below.

The tents of autumn corn spread far away,
stretch into desert.
Countless cities stand forgotten, empty, and
nobody moves through the streets.

Only ravens, shadows of the night,
fly under the thickening clouds in the rain.
Alone in the wind, like dark omens of sleep,
these black thoughts flee through wind-swept
hours.

Snow Crows

Black crows on a white field:
the sight clutches my heart. Snow flurries
encircle the world. Solemn crows sit and wait.

Magic birds from ancient times, they come to
visit us in gallows' clothes. The crime they wear
echoes the old curse.

A new spirit walks the forest but crows do not
see it move beside them in the whiteness
or hear it sound in winter woods.

Old crows cry out raw and hollow unhappy tales
of ancient worlds; they squat in the dark, and
snow swirls chill as night uncurls.

Migration Paths

These tracks have enchanted men a million
years, roadways moving birds high through the
sky. Like a ball of blue in a mist, the earth
turns as wings measure themselves against air.

The weight of men denies them these paths
refusing to lift cloven hooves, or paws.
No dust stirs there, no leaves fall from the
bough. If gods are there, they have no hair on
their brows.

From such a track in air above their heads men
see bird shadows break about their feet. The
beat of thin wings

uncovers the light they see flicker in the
lightning of the strokes.

Men have created bright metaphor;
the words have battered them with rough force.
Men's superficial magic chases birds along the
endless, invisible arch:

One end of the bridge rests in the frost where
sphagnum oozes and the owl circles and pumps
its feathered tail red from the rust gathered in
the stain of liquid iron.

At the other end the fish and insects hide, and
the greedy flock to this food and eat. The noise
of a moving stream resounds where the avian
road sinks in the sedge.

A journey brings birds to their winter feed
which heavy frogs and snakes or bears can strike
only if they fly to catch the soaring dream.
If only men had wings to take the paths of birds.

Fall Flight

"Todas la noche oyeron pasar pajaros" Columbus' Diary

"We heard birds in steady flight all night"—
myriad wings rustle through our dreams and

hide Orion from watchers on the roof who turn
their scopes north to the horizon,
and high southward without knowledge or
wisdom.

What calls birds to the skies on August nights,
who tells the thrushes and snipe to set forth
from forests and marshes; caged birds flutter.
What instincts move this nighttime armada? Jet
liners delay take of tonight; (All radar sets
flicker in confusion) pilots have to go to
bed or get drunk, controllers gaze from towers
with blind eyes into their cones of light that
shed no light—

the birds blip; all night long across the screen the
cormorant carries food in its pouch
for its young; golden eagles seek rabbits, a red
falcon clutches a quiet rodent,
while a griffon, long thought extinct, hunts lion
in the minds of watchers fed by radar.

Unseen birds grow larger, fiercer than those
seen. All night long the small songbirds and
shorebirds flash tiny silhouettes across the
moon;
for hundreds, thousands of miles their ceaseless
wings embrace the air and trouble dreams.

We study flight and learn migration paths, but
we will never lose Columbus' awe. What
threatens the skies in these latitudes
And what awaits us when these wings have
flown?

Ice Bird

A bird glides
through the vastness of space on unseen lines—
with the grace of a redbird
on a crockery face—

frozen and unheard
in the azure,
its wings undisturbed,

this flight is secure:
over blue ice
the dance is pure.

II

The beam in flight
to the radio set
pierces ears, a light

whose sound has fled
like a tone from struck glass

echoes in the head.

A silver tone can flash
over Calm Ocean
where hikers cannot pass.

The play of frost upon
the ice cuts with a harp
whose high note numbs

It's Spring Again

Two eggs, a loaf, a hat, and a hound— in spring
sky the white wool streams out, free
in a heaven without background.

So, uncultured friend, speak freely, and tell me
what I had.

Tell me what I was. A plough?
I had what I have now.
How do I know what I am? Fears?
So stupid, after sixty years.

A croaking raven,
I fly over my doubts and away. The wind
kidnapped my hound. The eggs, the bread, the
cognac taste good today. And look there: my old
hat makes little men and little paws.

Unicorn

A night wind
tugs at the heart;
it murmurs the bright art of spring.

In twilight treetops peacocks preen blue, golden,
green; and gray primates tumble, grin and snarl,
scuffle in the undergrowth.

A tiger crouches at wait,
lies low, watches, flashes its claws as bewildered
deer dart through the forest westward to the sea.

The unicorn's glee—zestfully his hooves battle
waves— deftly he runs with the hart and hunter.

Overhead dark cranes fly riddles in Arabian sky.
They offers us mirage with sinking sun— scarlet
apples, yellow pears, slices of ripe melon,
peaches, oranges, bunches of grapes.

Forts of amethyst, enchanted castles of topaz
and vermillion glow— rose mists flow
over a dark bay.
Unicorn day—
his hooves swirl
the soundless dust that furls
around minarets and gravestones.
They lie hushed

under a singing moon.
A night wind
tugs at the heart;
moon whispers the bright art of spring.

Unicorn eyes
embrace cold stars
and cities bleached for ghosts who hear the
desert owl,
the jackal howl, hyena laugh.
Beside old mud walls
under date palms
a bell calls
when a white dromedary lifts a calm head.

Move unicorn, move
unweighted feet
toward your fate;
your gaze glitters
like serpent eyes entranced
by the flute to untwine and dance.

The unicorn
runs in the night;
he carries high horn
with grace in his middle brow and sheds soft
light on uncovered face
and naked breasts
of the woman who waits to end his race.

She greets
him with her eyes
and murmuring lips, fountain—
night winds
tug at the heart;
they whisper the bright art of spring.

Flower Garden

Nothing else moves, no bird, no breeze,
a silver leaf flutters and whirls. Come with me,
girl, the dew-breathing grass lies cool like magic
on my feverish foot. Look around at our green
sea.

The great crested woodpeckers plunder nuts and
crack them.
Look there, they've drummed on that log. the
broken shells litter the ground,
but the birds are not calling now, the trees are
quiet.

Red apples flame upon the grass.
I try to shake of gold-green plums— I didn't
forget you, wait for me, please. I must ease my
hunger with fruit that fell from those empty
trees. What about you?

Can't you see butterfly peacocks light on the
rotten apple peel.
Hold me. We will sip like the butterflies who
draw the juice from fruit and reel— their colors
blind.

A mourning cloak spreads its velvet, purple
golden fringe, on that rose— stoop there and
smell. Yesterday it was only a bud;
the smell is sweet and pungent now.
Its odor charms.
Soon night will close upon the bloom, this
flower open now will die.
You know the hummingbirds and honeybees
must drink from out of flower mugs. Do bees
dream?

You will dream if you drink bees' milk,
sweet and creamy gold elixir. Loveliness spins
the handsome bees
that whirl, furious, hot-tempered skins into
swarms. Why do you look at me and laugh?
Do my eyes sparkle with your wine?
Will you laugh at my pulsing hand on your lips—
morning wind—soft swaying stalks, will we
drink in the sun?

Made of bronze, a tiny frog calls from water, and
a mermaid stirs,

freezes our blood, woman whose hair flows in
the pond, enchanting me.

We turn our faces from the bathers. If you give
me your flowing hair to ripple between my
fingers, will you mock me?

Like the growth on the river's bend, tender,
clasping camouflage— will you laugh?

The wind whispers your flight—
my fondling hands press soft plumage.
Are you the swan the great god of the ancients
took to create boy twins and Helen? Are you
Helen?

My eager hands smooth the feathers as broad
wings flash high symmetry. I understand ... I
dreamed...
a garden breathes when sun and rain enflame
the blooms for honey bees
and hummingbirds who taste the nectar.

Early Autumn

An insect sings
to the evening star.
The apples ripen
to their cores.

The treetops tire
from heavy fruit.
Fog climbs up high
to pasture.

Berries push themselves
against berries;
the bumblebee tells of aster honey.

A pear on the tree
matures and swells;
another pear
ripens and falls free.

I suck my cheeks full
of juice to dine
on the fruit
that offers first wine.

Curtain

When the mists creep
Like a night cloak
Over mountain rim
Through chestnut oaks

Then sounds grow dim
As the earth stills
For evening sleep.
It closes petals.

Sing, Katydid

A katydid sings, an unknown artist of the evening storms the heart. Memories of a kiss rush in the window where you rest an elbow and heavy thoughts.

You are there alone,
and the shadow image of our earth, the moon, comes secretly through the trees. That weird crone, the night, full of mirth and stars, takes little care of your despair ...

An eye is open still though it is deep night. On these shaking ramparts time passes.
Damp air makes you shiver, but soon it will be light. Then the solitary watch departs.
Life passes.

Memory

Years ago, each night
I was a pine tree
That clutched a cliff
To clasp the moon tight

With white hands.
Above the abyss
I bent in dance
And grabbed the mist
And clouds, my fleeting toys,
Above the steep rocks.
I feel no sorrow
Or wild delight, no joy,
When ecstasy fades
And pine bark sleeps
In deep shadow.

Jockeying Freeways

You jerk! You cut me of. You're real cool.
Get a nag in Tarquinia, driving fool!
In those tombs it is still the era of men,
The skies belong to birds, the seas to fish,
The earth to the bull and the noble horse.
Time here ticks of the folly of insects.

Or, have you covered up some secret news From
the tombs to the century of cars?
Then turn around, while the tunes of the dead
Still fend away the swarms of maenad bugs
And the scorn of apocalyptic hornets.
Drive down to the cities occupied

By pious age and guard the beautiful, The paintings, until the horn of morning Calls you to ride on a red Etruscan steed.
Too slow for you, though, you're such a sport.
Freeways demand more modern transport.

Jack-o-Lanterns

We've thought a long time
About jack-o-lanterns.
Sprightly aunts, they remind
Me of family concerns.

Between these clowns and me
There are close family traits
Few others have. Everyone can see
Us dance in the swirl of our race.

Yet I go where no pathways go,
Few men, in swaths of mist;
And I have watched winds blow
Closed the eyelids of dead artists.

Soul's Morning

An outcry from sleep
Creates a sense of deep
Sadness and cold, icy cleats
As winds retreat down dark streets
And circling stars undress

Their comeliness
In green rivers, silver alleys.
Towers gleam at new trees
As sun winks through
And drinks up purple dew.
Bluets spring out new dresses.
A quiet drunkenness
Moves a gliding boat.
Sun lovers gloat.
Songbirds pale
As lovers laugh and whirl
In children's garden worlds.
Primroses break the veil.

Gentian Blue

Here early snow sobs
Into moss mats.
Here knees throb
On steep paths.

The wind sings
A chill evening
To a child
Who asks why.

Gentian fall
Dares the first frost.
The flowers sprawl

Against rocks.

Sea drinks the small spring
Unseen in mountain thickets.
Only a salmon, dying,
Colors distress.

A gnarled fir
Still stands.
A mountain goat hangs
To cliff like a burr.

An old mountain,
An old strife,
The gentian
Comes under cold knife.

Ice and talus
Sleep and wait.
Only windy gusts
Awake.

A he-goat hurls
A bell on the wind.
A small girl
Grins.

A Child's Dream

Drunk with poppy juice and sad thrush note,
In silence, a bearded man touched woman.
His mother bore her child in a white moon
Under shadows of old maple trees.

In the soft window dark, old heirlooms
Lie in decay, old dreams of love can fall
Within father's moonlit ancestral vault,
Forgetful of cool breezes, green branches.

In dark days of his years, desolate childhood,
The boy imagined fishes swim cool streams
And threw himself down under horses hooves
Racing through black night as his stars seized
dreams.

He held the freezing hand of his mother
In the dusk as he crossed leaf-littered yards
When autumn brought a frail corpse to bed
In that dark room where he opened his eyes.

He was just a small bird in leafless trees.
In the shadow womb of the ancient trees
Bells rang at the stillness of his father
Who climbed down the winding stair to sleep.

He held the bony hand of the old man.
They went at dark to the falling walls

Of the city: a black overcoat dragged
The child to the maples; the ghosts approached.

Grasping green stuff of summer, how softly
The garden fell apart in autumn brown,
In scents of sadness from the old maples
When the boy heard the thrush and angels.

Silly Little Sun

My little sun ... when you rise in the sky you are
no bigger than a sparrow's head. Before the
cuckoo has three times told why, the clouds
with rain will wet our bed.

We are not supposed to see the blue dome then.
My brother, the wild tongue of the hound, sports
a blue flower, but who takes him home
for comfort under skies filled with summer
sounds?
What good comes from golden stars if
buttercups cannot counter the infertile
machine's shove and no maidens kneel to pick
blooms up to question if their lovers truly love?
What is the use of forget-me-not dares if the
girls ignore the wonders of sleep, staring their
dreams away like nightmares until their visions
turn and maidens weep away despair. My brain,
too, has fled from the warning calls of the rain-

bird nation: "You are no bigger than a sparrow's head when you rise in the sky, my little sun!

New Year's Eve

Through the turnip hole a mouse jumps
As wind breaks dry leaves from the oaks.
The hollow turnip gapes at stumps
While gusts whip the freezing dovecote.

Stout farm horses dress in long hair
Like wild beasts. The year comes and goes.
The oak falls, its cry lost in air
Like shouts over icy ocean floes.

Summer Crowd

Man-high wheat stands for harvest
Under a pale moon in twilight;
 The grain gloats at nightmare forest
Who listens in the dark night

The sickle mows the mass of gold,
The mower bathes in his motion,
The brown hands stretch and fold.
As feet edge forward mice run.
Who leads the cutter through the fields?

Why does wheat whisper in the furrows?

While the ears hear the wind rattle
And wail, the heads bend and bow.
Those that dare to speak mutter.

The billows of grain that strut the land
Rail at the lightning that kills them,
But they are stretched out by its hand
And their wide field becomes sodden.

Where have the golden days all gone?

The crowd whispers we are here still.
No one believes happy days will end
Though the sickle sounds a high peril.
Each stalk hears and trembles and bends.

One night the sickle strikes this place
Under bright stars and batwings.
The nightmare makes a cunning face
At the stalks. He knows what frost brings.
Who ponders where the guys have gone?

Old Raven

I saw a bird
Long years ago, heard
His croaks near old gray towers
In London.
He told that travel sours.

It had undone
Him.
He sat black and hopeless.
Legend says
He sat there speechless
Hour after hour
And watched old kings' treasure
In the tower
Year after year.
Today I know
The meaning of that dream, Its power.
I have felt regret
And seen that bird again.
I have seen inside the tower
At night and know
What wealth he watched.
Lying worn, I heard Him say his truth,
"Lost, youth."

Winter Moonlight

I watch February moon lie
On clear heaven, turquoise-blue.
In winter grasses, yellow fire,
Sheep move and rest and chew.

The ram aches for beauty's ewe.
Wool gleams star-cleansed coral.
I know the words to raise the moon:

I am in Paradise before the Fall.

Summer Seaside

A napping cat is not undone
by hot stones or noise from a house whose clock
and stereo sounds
prompt noonday dreams as sea soaks sun.

Bathers on the beach burn asleep, have lost the
world and do not care that smells of sea or sand
they wear sprint with the sea wind from the
deep.

Empty space creates cloud cities while wavering
heat waves massage skies' freckled gull and tern
montage whose muted cries cause no unease.

Across the summer heat birds fly and light on
the fishermen's stakes. Dark thunderheads begin
to make, yet threatening clouds escape hot eyes.

Ash Wednesday

Yesterday I wore rainbow scarves
Through peacock, singing worlds.
Today my desire starves,
Its peacock plumes all furled.

One eye looks back that way
The other looks on dearth.
Quickly, suddenly, flower earth
Shows me no blooms today.

The moon is yellow, flat, untrue.
The skies are cold and blue,
My wood lies under icy stars,
Its peacocks all departed.

September

You, who lean on the fence in front of phlox and
oaks (splattered by rainstorm and the scent of
wild beasts) who like to walk the stubble and
talk to the old folks gathering juicy autumn apple
feasts,
you breathe on the fields smoking with heated
foggy cloaks.
You lack the will that snow and winter bring to
yell, "Hey, you're wasting time,"
at the vines climbing up. The summer workers
sing; you restrain your voice. Workers chime,
"You're short and fat and heavy-set,
rotten pumpkin beside your shoe, wet
fungus without face, slimy growth and grime."
Climber from the plains, flames from a final
moon swelling out fever and fruit, drooping face
already dark— knave or fool or baptizer,

idiot of summer, clattering echo, death rattle,
crooner of morning song of glaciers, brush-
cutter, nut-cracker, adage-eater, shark.
In front of you lie snow, high silence, and barren
space without plants: your long arm reaches
there, yet you lean over the fence as beetles
throng among the greens—
all life eats life—spiders and field mice and hares
and autumn leaves are chewed by winter scenes.

Last Day of Summer

Day, you end the summer games.
Your signs all fall apart
And set of forest flames,
Autumn hues that tug the heart.

After you, pictures turn pale
And snatch at the cold times.
Water glistens like flat ale
Even though waters are wide.

You must learn how to fight
And battle to slow your flight,
To which the swarms, the crowds,
The armies of ice bring shrouds.

Snowflakes

Slowly turning green limbs white, nothing
speaks with greater softness: like lovers
whispering low at night, who sleep together in
their strangeness and in the morning's
brightening light find an odd earth has built for
their delight a nest full of celestial whiteness.

Comic Fall

The clusters of grapes
ripen clear through;
frost transforms green shapes with dreamlike
hues as winds weave light.

Leaf after leaf falls
to dust the lawn;
a white hand mauls
the woodland thorns
as trees strip bare.

The hounds and hunters cry what life has
breath.
The dead year's drunken hires bequeath what's
left with absurd hope.

Laughing, the first snow gleams on
mountainsides.
Bird flocks dull its glow but cannot hide

the silver course of death.

Spring Rack

A fish in a brown sea of cognac, my corpse
swims with white belly firm, intact. From the
drunken sack on my skeleton, laurel grows.

I have reached the revelry of grave, a drunken
ghost among spring roots whose drinkers dance
into my mound— from out of my heart the
laurel grows.

Burgundy red streams from my pores, the
restless vines spring out of me while mustard
seed sprout in my ears— from out of my chest
the laurel grows.

Blue eyes lengthen on the larkspurs, tips of
buffalo grass grow pale
as hungry moles grub in my stomach— from out
of my groin the laurel grows.

Drunken riot resounds the earth, the worms that
feast my body's core have broken down the
bones to dust— from out of my loam the laurel
grows.

Birding with the Bard

I. To Verona

Journeying west, we hope to see the bard; the
birds, and a country called America— like a sea
journey, though earth's hard core grounds our
quest for celestial liquor.

We are almost self-contained, pared to bone; in
our truck we stow food and sleeping gear so that
we can see wild lands red-bone raw between
those nights we soak up Shakespeare.

Trip to give art and nature time to heal
the pain in my side and the ache in my head.
Ventures in art and nature's art I feel
will weigh against desire to wake the dead and
tell them that they cannot tie my heart to a rack
of memories, marriage woes
of lovers of an old form grown apart visited to
the second generation:
a roadside lark lifts its voice in a pose suggesting
a songbird's celebration.

Tonight we look into curio dens offered
charitably to men and women who try to stay
cool in the evening heat. We read the welcome
banners on the street.

Tonight we shall see the *Two Gentlemen*,
tomorrow *Romeo and Juliet*—
we mix birds and bard in a westward trek begun
in Elizabethan 'Bama
where red elephants vie with high drama for
those whose entertainment reeks of sex.

The arts can flourish under a big tent before
their patrons have learned discontent.

Bald spot floodlighted on Romeo's head does
demand disbelief over dismay
to think him young and yet so hairless. We can
accept our youthful heroes bald with power of
strong imagination.

We make far greater imaginary leaps imagining
touchdown runs heroic. Consider, what is an
instant replay but aesthetics shown the athletic
way?

There was a time I remember yet when ardent
nightingales sang all night for me, young Romeo,
and Juliet.

Having spent an evening and matinee with
Alabama's answer to Stratford
-on-Avon, we turn our trucking bed and board
westward toward the Father of Waters.

At Vicksburg we pause to honor the dead on the
bluff above old father's voyagers. My son cannot
easily understand why the brochures offers
little quarter to the Confederate dead. Bloody
hands still wave bloody shirts in federal words.

The monuments seem to echo the curse of
separate blood. "Why do the Yankees have all
the big memorials?" he asks.

"The victors get the tombs and eulogies."

Memories of feuding Capulets
and Montagues fresh in our mind's eye we watch
the river below us; we vet, surrounded by
monuments to fratricide— marble wavers in
bright light, clownish like the balding spot our
Romeo showed under the merciless spotlight's
beams. Union, Confederate sorrows made
dreams sweet with grief for novelists and
movies.
Warblers and wrens chant hymns in the
thickets, celebrate blue and gray with equal zeal:

the cuckoo's elegiac rain dirge peals against the
light engulfing all hard tombs in the heat...
chants for passionate debris.

Flight
moves through beatitudes and eons—
thin-winged
meteor gray bird slips
through air thick with afternoon heat waves,
A Mississippi kite seeking snakes,
swoops down and eyes us— flips over the ridge
to soar in blue-ringed clouds above the river,
flies into thunderheads— melding with sky
like my first Mississippi kites on the Savannah
that :fed into high ceiling, free:
This bird we share expands in time beyond my
ken.

II. The Big D

Across high asphalt of a river bridge
the land lies flat nine hundred miles or more
before the rocks rise up from desert brush to
foretell the Rocky Mountain ridges.
Open air, damp commodious tile marks water
spots unlike those pioneers sought
to slake their greater thirst on westward treks.
Cactus wrens and western kingbirds drink here,

too, and they and the Crissal Thrashers yell as
gold wings flash in manzanita hell
to set brush on fire and warm tile glaciers.

Along the Dallas freeways we seek theater—
Shakespeare's shrew will play the Texas sky.
Nighthawks skim above us, cowboy boots
promenade before us, giving Mantua
a sagebrush :favor to match the stucco stage that
Katharina treads in cowgirl style: so we are
come abroad to see a world as hot as Petruchio's
Italy—
the dry air cools to aid the wooing fight.

O slanderous world! these Texas artists are apt
as those of London to hold our gaze in thrall. No
curtains mark
this thespian feat: we share Hortensio's shock
the shrew is tamed with Dallas girls; they walk
the aisles, discreet.

Interstate, desert brush, and blue sky patched
with fluffy clouds flash by, flash by— the hot
Texas plains stretch out before us
a long carpet with lots of brush—design broken
here and there with the apparatus of oil wells,
some resting, some on line, pumping
rhythmically, black seesaws
working to raise their quota of dollars.

In the distance the shine of El Paso
gleams below the ridge, beckons...Rockies Ho!

Birds circle the ridges (swooping swallows)
towering above—red and blue, rainbows to egg
on heated, dry- mouthed travelers toward cool,
clear waters of old stories.

"What's that blue streak that flew through the
air?" We stop and look in trees under the bridge
to find a male Blue Grosbeak preening there.
Looking at the high peaks ahead, I think of a
fellow who laughed at the ridges
of eastern mountains. "You call those
mountains? Why those are just foothills. Now
the Rockies, they rise up and let you know
they're there.
I tell you we've got lots of hills back home
bigger'n these ant bumps covered with hair."

III Arizona Peaks and Deserts

When I see them rise in clear desert air these
peaks do dwarf tree-clad Appalachians. Those
forested hills we left behind
are filled with warblers now, exuding birds red,
blue, and yellow—dots of feathers glow against a
green sea of rainforest leaves.

Here we see a different wilderness. The
Chiricahuas loom ahead. Cactus
flowers paint hot, rocky hillsides yellow
and red and green. We ride through hot canyons
where ocotillos raise their spindly arms
and climb steep, winding roads eight thousand
feet to Rustler Park, where we camp for a week.
Events do not fulfill advance billing.
No rustlers are here in the seventies.
We bird and await Shakespeare in Utah.

The little meadow below the campground is an
enchanting spot that turns blue with iris in May
and delphiniums in August, both attracting
hummingbirds broad-tailed and rufous—jewels
stun birders' eager eyes that follow their :faming
hues.

We wake at early dawn and look for birds before
we bathe with water from the one campground
spigot (what is termed a sponge bath is not
immersion but it does cut dust). Red-shafted
flickers and western bluebirds
and red-faced warblers decorate our morning.
Robins, boldly ubiquitous, make us feel at home,
but huge ponderosa pines alive with Olive and
Grace's warblers let us know this is a new world

entered. When we descend into Cave Creek Canyon, we find elf owls and gray-breasted jays to complement dainty painted redstarts in trees where truly elegant trogons nest in old Arizona sycamores.

The time comes to power our yellow truck toward Patagonia, the roadside stop where many reports of marvelous birds originate: rare Rose-throated Becards, Beardless Tyrannulets, Thick-billed Kingbirds. Outsiders are fenced out from the dude ranch but do not have to chance trespass. Becards have hung their nest just beside the highway where every passer-by can take a look.
This doesn't include the dude who creeps through wayside in a green Jaguar in first gear, one hand on the wheel, the other flipping through Jim Lane's guide to Arizona birds. It is rare to see birders such as he
looking as if they've just stepped from a page of Jim Bean's catalog. Three-thirty-three— the desert birds are quiet except for that gem, the lazuli bunting serenading me.

An old school bus sits in the wayside park. It's still there when the evening turns to dark.

Old man in a bus
a long way from Tennessee talks about hard
times and his woman
who matches his social security check
and grey hair
with hers.
The heat of Patagonia never forces his lady to
eject from their yellow earthcraft. "Four days
we've been here," he says
and leaves us to imagine what sanitation on that
bus is like.

Fleeing heat, we seek Madera Canyon
by way of Ramsey Canyon hummingbirds. We
pay our fee and sit in the lawn chairs casually
placed among a myriad
of feeders that hang from many limbs and dare
birds to visit for public stares. Magnificent green
hummingbirds attend two feeders. A blue-
throated stakes a claim determinedly to one
before my face.

Madera Canyon brings adventures
with odd owls and sparrows and goshawks.
Beside a motored camper we hear owls whose
bleat confuses tenderfeet.

The western screech owl repeats his howl long
enough for us to figure out

he's not just another misplaced easterner.

Later we hike up a steep slope to find the
whiskered owls that inhabit here.
In full moonlight we hear the sound and peer
into the trees where the boo *boo boo...boo* seems
to originate. Our luck has changed,
who missed the wary Flammulated Owls along
the Chiricahua Barfoot Trail, flushed out before
us in our daytime treks and rained away from
owl hunts at night.

In daylight we climb up Madera slopes
to find a brown-throated wren singing out to
lure us up and up. When we head down we thrill
to see swift flight of a goshawk descending
before us. At the trail's end
we hear screams of distress along the stream and
run to find a young Cooper's Hawk in the
clutches of the larger goshawk.
We interfere with the ecosystem
and the Cooper's Hawk flies back to the nest.

In the bright sunshine of Floreeda Gulch we look
among the brush, grass, and cacti
for rare Rufous-winged Sparrows. They are
there and flush long enough to make us happy.
Their color's drab, but rareness paints them fair.

A Tucson gem is the Desert Museum where we
can see rare cacti and rare birds before we
ascend Mt. Lemon high above the sweltering
saguaro heat.
Here cool streams and trees amaze us—this
place cools us the way the U-Totem ice cools
our food. Mountain breezes delight our faces.
The guidebook agrees this air blows cooler—
it's cold as ice a few miles higher up when we
climb from saguaro cactus flats into the pinyon
oaks as dusk brightens city lights thousands of
feet below us. The breeze at eight thousand feet
tightens our skin a bit. We put on coats, move
out, and camp. We light our labor with starlight.

Next morning we hike out to see the sights. We
revel in profusion of flowers
and the belligerence of a Broad-tailed
Hummingbird who has staked an angry claim to
flowery roadside. He hurls his power
at those who test. He plays no favorites between
us, broad-tails, or golden eagle soaring overhead,
brown god of the heights, who returns our eager
gaze with sharp eyes.

We take the lift up to the mountain top and loaf
under the ponderosa pines

while clownish Tassel-eared Squirrels define us
as dangerous. The mother removes
her young from their hiding place to find other,
safer spots. Squirrels take babies from forest
spire to forest spire of fir.

Before we descend the slope on the lift a
western tanager bares bright beauty, black and
yellow and red, flaring in sky. Eyes spot the
Golden Eagle soaring high
above. Adrenalin excites the mind and
binoculars sharpen our weak eyes
as the brown-winged god circles overhead,
climbs, then stoops with grace below the ridge.

When we arrive at Aravaipa Creek
the desert heat seems dry and bearable. Along
the creek we feel humidity.
The heat clutches cactus and jeers at us. We
slump under a cottonwood whose girth
announces centuries of sunny earth
and life-giving water drawn from the creek.

Bushtits
and vermillion flycatchers :fit from twig to
twig— they wear a gaudy rig
that seems to turn up the heat.
The black hawk screams, "If you can't stand the
heat get out of my canyon."

He does not soar at mid-day but stays over the
stream and laughs at me—in his cool and
rippling pool I collapse
and gulp for breath beside fast waters.

IV Utah Arts

Quickly black thunderheads roll from the west
announcing time for hasty departure.
We are not fast enough. From summer heat the
landscape changes—the jagged lightning
preludes the deluge and slippery roads. We slide
to stop and wait under eerie
night in day, wondering where dryness went,
thinking forward to the heath where Macbeth
would hear the Utah witches prophesy.
Later we head north to Cedar City through the
pines of northern Arizona whose top peaks
testify to rainfall high enough to grow trees
three hundred feet tall. Brian's Head lies on his
great rocky bier

in Utah. The Indian chief has lain prone to the
skies for centuries. Recently, his repose has been
taken in vain
by sightseers who desecrate his bones. Brian
weeps rocks into valleys below while wind-torn
pines stoop in his cheeks to form his hairline.
Hordes of red finches, pepper red, Cassin's

scatter like dandruff among the trees. From his
eyebrows we peer into the red rocks— pimples
of his face offers primitive carvings in sunburst
exploding when clouds shift their embrace over
arena of the Great Spirit.
The great chief weeps and sighs at the smog
blowing eastward from the Kaiparowits.
The ghosts of the Anasazi dogs
howl their lament from the Kaibab plateau
to sandstone winds and waters carved to form
great obelisks to awe the Navajo.

Measure for Measure marks our first foray to
Cedar City.
The motel gives us a chance to wash grime of the
trip away before we seek the solace of the bard.
Unfortunately married Claudio, lovely Isabel,
lusting Angelo rival Brian's red finches and blue
grouse.
I feel pain in my side begin to grow
as Mistress Overdone's lust brings down the
house.

Next day at Lava Point among aspen
the sky-blue mountain bluebird sings to us while
eagles soar above yellow-headed blackbirds
outsinging pond frogs and bees. The black-
chinned sparrows in the chaparral of lower
slopes brighten evening pall

but the sudden breeze makes quaking aspens
rustle under a full moon and bend
in the firelight. *Unglaublich!* German speech
floats to us —bits on the wind in the trees from
flickering campfires neighboring ours lending a
mildly cosmopolitan touch to wildness. Dry
branches spark in the heart.

The Green River country must have caught its
name from imagination, or envy green
at humid Colorado ground above.

Again we pursue Shakespeare—in Cedar City
lights. This night noble Macbeth bleeds for us—
tainted by a bad director
who cannot decide whether the lady is for
burning hell or just a happy housewife helping
her husband get ahead.

V Colorado High

The land we move quickly through next day is
land where solitary ravens play
a desperate game. The careful descent to
Colorado could cause some heartburn for those
drivers who must go slow or burn out brakes.
Runaway truck ramps astonish us— one safety

spot ends in sheer rock wall and another leaps
out over a gorge. Ravens gather
at rabbit kills on the road.
Like Odin's dead rabbit corpses wear raven
shrouds at dusk.
Most perching birds
depend on husks
of camouflage
or minute size
to hide their fear.
Ravens
find black
a hue that suits t
heir oracular act.
Grand Mesa rises against the parched plain,
whose beauty we have to hurry through with
only a stop or two to complain about green grass
and water rising up over a parched land where
even a Raven marauding must carry his own
grub.
In Mesa Verde foothills magpies cavort
in trees that shade the cattle from the sun.
Arlechino—
O fortunate eye
to behold these magpies
on the foothills of Mesa Verde cavorting on
fence lines and trees and cow pods, a context
that defines the rustic loafing at ease, raucous,
loud, chatter ironic—

unlike those city ‘pies we later see high
over the golden arches, black-billed magpies
burnt by setting sun—they fly above
MacDonald’s. I take their silence for disdain of
Boulder’s traffic. The scene is hardly sylvan— a
metropolitan frieze in which aboriginal clowns
act solemn.

At dark the yellow-bellied marmots sing their
siren song on rocks of Loveland Pass. Their
melodious squeals and grunts ring dulcet sounds
to listening ears, alas.

Two human sirens, fishers, join our camp to hear
what spirits haunt the rocky cliffs.
Their struggle raises tent and roasts some
trout— hails sweet marmot song with unsteady
shouts. They are quiet when morning marmot
whistles and white-crowned sparrows wake us
from sleep made fitful by the thinness of the air.

Awake, we rise and push on to Boulder—
Byron, Hal and Hamlet wait for us there
and we celebrate each night with Shakespeare,
glorify days with Rocky Mountain birds.
The flatland fields north of city cement offers us
elegant western grebes on ponds and Lewis’
woodpeckers in cottonwoods. The evening
shows scenes of war and peace in open air

where swifts swarm before dark descends its
curtain to engulf our minds with Love's Labor's
Lost: I create an arc that links the pain in my
side to the blind web of necessity that wrecks
acted feast.

The oxygen at fourteen thousand feet on Mt.
Evans, rarer still, can impair
the lungs and brain. Here too marmot grunts
enhance the meadow flowers, summer fare for
marmotry. They harvest tundra hay and whistle
while they work in rocky lairs.

The blue grouse with her chicks crossing the
road heralds good fortune. Hammond's
flycatcher calls to us on the trail through
evergreens
at nine thousand feet, "I'm here, birdwatchers."
Rocky Mountain high—traffic jams blue sky of
Paradise.
Motors hum as drivers look for places to park.
The signs order,
"Don't feed the birds," but gawking tourists
thrive on giving handouts to Clark's nutcrackers.
They cast their bread into the air, up high, to
watch the gray-black birds do barrel rolls.

At Medicine Bow the rosy finches sit on dirty
snow to pose for pictures. Following faint trails

through rocky tundra we look and find a white-
tailed ptarmigan whose camouflage permits a
secret plan that does not include
flushing from her nest among the gray rocks—
except under duress.

We salute the sky, our father, We caress the
earth, our mother. We acknowledge our cousins
the flowers of the tundra. Throughout the
meadow we search for our sister, the ptarmigan,
whose gray caress coheres with the rocks,
her softness set in volcanic stone.
Her grey feathers mock
but dress the rocks.

She flies at me with desperate wings
when I stomp upon rocks close to nestlings.
In the Pawnee Grassland we spend the night in
the truck, hearing hoots from owl burrows. They
deride our missing Crow Valley Park. Too tired
to take offense, we take delight and fall asleep by
counting their barks.

Next day we savor some longspurs, McCown's
and Chestnut-sided, and trace these birds down
in plowed fields where they are easily seen.
At a prairie pond dried almost to mud we stop to
gaze at a gathering flock of shorebirds, where
Cedric Foster

and his grandson park their pickup, unlock the
gate and ask us in for closer looks.
We close enough to identify Baird's Sandpipers
among the peeps probing there.

North to the Oregon Trail we follow roads as
straight as those across the coastal plain though
we are five thousand feet above sea with flat
land around us. We turn again at the interstate
and start heading east.

Descending fast from Colorado high, we journey
to join the River Platte
serenaded by raven laughter, wry.
The first-year chase,
belly roll and :fail
a strut before a sleeping pal
and a tug on the tail—
the race is on.
Ravens vault the air
and tumble there with free falls,
raucous calls
inviting all
to the game.
A test of will,
a means of release,
a complex way
to learn survival skills.
Fond of play,

ravens will perform,
even caged
will entertain themselves
with mime.
Enclosed,
his acrobatic pose
slides down
a smooth perch,
his posture
like an otter's
upright in his lurch—
little boy buoyant
whose mirth totters
solemn cant.
Iron bars
cage performance,
not the dancing heart.

VI Homeward Bound

The distance east we travel fast to meet the
silver arch towering St. Louis
and barely reach the mounds across the river in
time to see tree sparrows well enough
to put them on the list. They are tougher to find
than we expected, but we meet before dark
blears binocular vision.

In Louisville we stop for Shakespeare's *Merry*
Wives of Windsor, a nightly feat
in the park, where the bard embraces deer in
sylvan surroundings fitting for Falstaff wearing
woodland horns that make him fear
his band of malcontents, who bring us laughter
—wring our minds back to mundane careers.
I long to ask Falstaff what provoked him to his
mid-life folly. "Why play the fool?

Why do they call it the mid-life crisis? It
happens to people of all times
and not at some predetermined stasis." The
question does not identify a crime but all the
same implies a falling off, at least a mildly
inoffensive cough
They all fall from grace though they avoid grime.

Who is they? The holders of what? That jizz
known as community standards? It is their call.
They term it infidelity
and go on talk shows for celebrity.

Careless illicit loves succumb to guns
or tongues. What sins cannot neighbors detect?
Running around on one's mate is not done
boldly, with an honest
flouting of rules.

The righteous require a decent respect for
propriety. Those who ignore rules must be
cleverly subversive, not fools.

The pain in my side gnaws against my mind, a
warning birds and bard can only wind
temporary spells. Their magic may not last to let
me subdue the patriarchal past unless
imagination allows me
to fasten mime to timeless imagery.
Tomorrow we make our circle just
at home now that we've slaked our wanderlust.

With and Without Love

Malt, Milton, and Mary Jane

It's on the house,
the keg carried from room to room is a broom
to sweep away thoughts
that make us believe our life is real.
The warmth of flesh is a reality
we find by putting one finger against another,
the mesh of touching actuality.

Sleek hips and delicate white arms, five-pronged
silver forks wet with the beer they serve,
a freshly painted carriage
covered tightly with a plastic wrap,
impressed elasticity of patterns
etched in symbolic tracery of clock
with lines of black and red.
Underneath, the whiteness of pillows and ships
sailing and under this the electric aliveness of
animal azure eyes in token of the sea

and the star-nippled sky; The whirling shadows
rest on inundated skin. a ring to be worn
sapphire and golden in sensuous glow.

A sheet woven bright for a dance of no finality
lies on her smile;
a vinyl curtain quickly drawn, the temporary to
die serves the drinks.

Morning Song

Nestled in weary arms she warms my chest with
youth and laughter against the coming dawn,
when emptiness embraces her.

Counting days and nights
before her lips laugh in my eyes
like holiday lights,
she numbers memories
with sighs.

Recalling how we part
she begs me, "Stay,
oh, do not rise;
the day breaks not, it is my heart"-light shining
from her eyes overpowers art.

The anguish of the heart
is not confined to her face alone;

my joy must die apart
from her sweet tones
of love by loss refined.

Night Winds

The African night
settles over acacia trees
leaving me no light
to erase memories.

When the day birds still,
passions no longer quell their cries.
They swell up until
my flesh escapes mind's hide.

Then fever trees
outline on a dark sky designs
whipped by night breeze for lovers and lions.

Another Opinion

This churning in the gut
is not what
lovers write about
when they tout
bright love in song.

The loneliness, the ache— the fears that break
out in cold sweats—

I think you will forget
our song of love.

Then memories calm.
They are a balm
to heal doubt's wounds: cherish quiet hours,
croons my troubled mind.

Chiropractor's Dream

I diagnosed my moon girl
a harlequin some days before she complained of
a backache. She fell in a swoon
as she sat in my waiting room.

That beauty moon
slipped her disk.
I tried to relieve her with runes rubbed against
her back while I chanted
ancient spells as I tuned her body's vertebrae
rack.

She didn't like the treatment, and she flipped.

When she ran, I chased her
over the fields until she slipped
and did not stir as I pressed her hips
against the fur
of our mother's skin.

I massaged and lipped
my moon girl's myrrh
as she lay under the stars where she had tripped
upon her soft and hidden cares until the sun
awoke and stripped
the shadows of our moon world.

Bloodline

On telephone wire above clean water a
kingfisher watches for his prey— for fish in
creek, and us, no quarter.
September heat envelops landscape
whose virgin old growth was made conquest to
render the fat of Boone's land, a rape.

Ridge and valley fell to ax wielded by pioneer—
nature could not deny
this great urge that stirred her rocky fields.

This place where we attempt escape of ancient
design lies in sunshine that ripens patriarchal
landscape.

September sun heats my gaze. It gleams
into ageless eyes—kingfisher plunges,
wings folded, beak straight, into clear stream.

Horizons beckon—movement in dreams— we
drain from heights to mountain valley. Our high
desire runs down with the stream.

Silver Linings

We sit and talk,
students who catch flies
or God
upon the pen's point,
impalers and impaled,
we balk
at selling the old lies
with which we're shod
to beg the point.
Old Socrates,
you cry against
our sophistry and poetry and fees:
your students followed free, Plato's disease.
With pen and chalk
or hemlock talk
we rap,
we breeze
to grease the laugh
of Aristophanes.

We sense
the mystery of winds,
Aeolian harps,

high recompense for sin.

Retreat

They talked,
the two from prison
returning home.

One man
told how he'd been
a long time away

From the taste
of woman
and white liquor.

The other man
said hell would crack
before he went back

To the arms
of lawmen
who'd see you sweat, or hanged.

The bus carried them
over the black asphalt
of Camp Thirteen.

Foxtrot

necks bend
as backs sway
got corn
to hoe today
breezes blow
big clouds by
some low
some up high
warm earth
meets the sky
what a shame
we dance to die.

The Catch

Sunspots flickered leaves as the chameleon
glittered in my garden
and slowly blinked his lizard eyes before two
grimy hands encircled leather.
My pride of parenthood
was mixed with awe to see
the anole turn from green
to red to brown within
the lizard-catcher's hands—
my son's delight in turning suns. How swiftly
anoles run among the summer leaves— those
hands that deftly hemmed the lizard have caught
age,

but I am still amazed to think of anoles turning
green to beige and green again.

Yamaha Use

Vrooommm ...
Over the yellow buttercups I walk outside
to meet my son announcing with regard
how I, in my name for insurance, own a
motorcycle I must ride
at least five percent
of the time.
So I am bent
unwilling mime's
affinity to Hell's Angels
and must tacitly approve
an incarnation
of Evil Kneevil ringing his bell as he hits the
groove
in my back yard churning the buttercups,
Vrooommm ...

Creon, I Have Met You

In modern Thebes old Creon walks to see we
leave the dead in fear;
he walks with lengthened face and balks at
seeing souls cross Charon's pier.

The ancient man still mocks the gods (or has he
clear forgotten them?) who still demand the
turning sods for eyes that weaken and grow dim.

He has forgot the fate of man,
of Jocasta and his brother;
he lives in Thebes as he began,
rejecting God and sepulcher.

Needed: Pharaoh's Daughter

A happy infant should glow
healthy and full of joy—
strong in the life force that grows
from digested lactose. Boy

or girl, love does not question the future role of
diapers, genetic replication.
Love presses its warmth to fur.

The baby in a hovel burgeons happily at breast
that's quickly near, picks up well soon after the
squalling test.

Suburbs create marasmus neglectful as
tenements. The careless bottle can crush— cold,
affluent negatement.

Ackerman's Laugh

Ackerman, the sharp young archeologist, stood
in a cave in Borneo and looked about him at the
walls and read the list of Vedic heroes' graven
there by crooked, gnarled hands that believed in
legend.

You gods, he thought, could not keep your
friend alive; he's been dead these twelve
hundred years. Ackerman almost doubled up at
this. He grinned up at the idols. His face burst
into tears at the thought of this ironic, ageless
joke.

He laughed and laughed until he seemed to
choke, until the silent cave began to grumble.
As Ackerman stood there in his witty glow the
ground beneath his feet began to rumble and
idols tumbled
down on merry foe.

911: Final Call

Her dark hair in curlers
and delicate fingertips
amazed the men who found her
sleeping with blue lips near her baby's bassinet
arrayed in pink and white to match the bright
flowers on the table she had set for her guests

that night— she had arranged for hours. Her
dried curls depressed as they pulled her fresh
from the kitchen range, her unaccustomed
stiffness marked her change
toward formality. Surrounded by her last valets
she cried less strenuously about the empty days
of matrimony.

The Door-to-Door Show

Reel I: Sampling

Home from school, looking for a job to heal the
wings of a young bird fallen in flight, crashed out
of college life onto the streets of harsher
reality—winging retreat, an owl returns with his
sorrow toned
to the shade of the arching trees of home,
desiring a Bo- Tree in Virginia ... contemplation
beneath clouds of regret—

with clear eyes Guy sees the need to get a stake:
the want ad reads, "We want a clean-cut man,
personable, young, seeking a career
in advertising. Salary plus expense account.
Apply Montisello Hotel
in room two at nine o'clock on Monday."

No longer there, a Greek revival building torn
down with difficulty to raise up bare-sided walls,

straight lines of modernity cast against pigeons
and valued beauty—

it is there on application day
in June of '53: Guy's plodding ways
begin at eight on Tuesday, on the pavement,
walking the streets, following the chalk the
leader marks to organize
Guy's walk.

He sees American birds answer the door or fly
away to hide a body bathed
in startled agitation, like the lady Aphrodite of
the ironing board
who gives him, his youthful eyes, a vision of
American beauty in the flesh, nude, raising his
temperature and humidity already sweltering in
the Norfolk heat.

She appears from the half-light of the screen,
standing at her steaming board, her back to him,
hip curved to the thrusting line of the board,
Venus Callipygous sways to her work.
Casually planted pelvis swings with the work
until the doorbell rings and the nude turns to
greet him, expectant, lover awaited, aglow with
the blondeness of her pubic hair and the mane
flowing blonde to her elbows.

Her breasts lift toward him, the nipples greeting
him before she snorts and shrieks her dismay
uncovered to Actaeon eyes burning her body.
Aphrodite flies away from glance of boy who
offers coupons instead of the love she expected.

Consider how Tom impaled his Godiva.
What if Eve had flown from the serpent
whose gaze must have surprised her with its
glint?

Reel II: Pounding Pavement

From his wagon the leader enforces the soap.
Sample deliveries, coupons to whet the needs of
America's wives:

"We are the boys from P & G
who trek our souls through city streets.
Housewives, hold out your hands and take our
treats. Don't fly away from us like scared
pigeons." Despair, decay, beautify a summer day.

Guy passes by blocks of rubble renewal— knock
at a ghetto door gets sultry voice: "Coupons for
you lady; here you are"— "Come on in white
boy, come into my room

and let me show you a good time."—"No, thanks,
but here's coupons with our compliments."

Ebony skin invites, water steams
in stagnant pools, odors of stale urine and bacon
grease fried earlier that day mix with the spoor
of dogs in the mire.
Sex and nostrils assailed, Guy notices pools
covered with oil slick, shining in sunshine, all
the rainbow colors broken apart.

Two blocks over on Boush Street he knocks on
the door. Short and brown, a warbler in disarray
waves Guy into her room with ill grace, a
deadpan comedienne. She is confounded when
he offers
soap coupons instead of sex—she smiles and
smiles into mirrors without a back ...
a bed, some pictures on dimly lighted walls... she
puts her hand upon his arm and sings,

"Coupons? Boy, now that's just what I need."
Well, Guy agrees, of course, and P & G
triumphs ... a gentle Christ beams down on
things.
His youthful amazement complements her aloe
gaze, her saffron smile, her scent.
The dirty tenements, row upon row, invite
Guy's feet to starlings and sparrows that glare at

him from houses peeling paint as they await the
crews to tear them down for urban renewal. He
climbs the steps.

Weathered boards betray yellow paint, tearing,
chipping of, unable to wait for the chain
and ball of destruction smashing its way along
the street toward the water's rim. The gulls
wheeling overhead cry his pain.

He stops upon the sagging porch and knocks at a
gaping doorway, then enters the hall, hesitant,
moves slowly past more doors,
all of them open to his eyes ... feet forward ...
slowly, slowly ... Guy falters to vision.

So peacefully she lies there spread-eagled on the
rumpled bed covered with her body and one
sheet, Aphrodite asleep,
curves akimbo, her silken hair, reddish blonde,
curling under her arms and at her crotch— she
doesn't use peroxide for her beauty ... a beatific
face betrays no sign of weariness, no lines, no
petulance
in the open lips that frame white teeth ... even in
their slight smile they deceive:
wet beauty adorning an ugly crib.

The mounted Venus grins at men as though, lips
parted, slightly moist, a passive dove awaits the
ever-expected kiss.

Reel III: Westward Ho!

At appointed minute the caravan
lurches into dawn, moving south and west,
snaking out on the highway to Statesville to join
other wagons heading west.

Night in a cheap hotel gives Guy time to study
color plates of birds, paeans
to beauty that he fears won't sing or soar.

In two days flight Guy reaches plains of grass
and scissor-tailed flycatchers sitting fence beside
golden dickcissels throating song.

The too-drab plates in Guy's old Peterson do not
describe the beauty that he sees. The landscape
they travel into Texas reminds Guy now of that
Childe Roland rode toward the Dark Tower. The
cattle skulls offset a lazuli bunting's song
and a ladder-backed peckerwood flying in front
of the car to shouts of surprise—

in the Big D guys lose virginity:

the elevator man pimps, and Lew haggles him
down for Guy. Later, after enough booze, Guy
sees the girl come
in the room, undress and climb upon his bed.
Her expertise staves of disaster, and she stuffs
him in at the black hair that does not match her
head.

Long after, Guy wonders what the pleasure was.
Across the border from El Paso,
down the dusty street—the wide, wide street of
yellow dust that leads to Mexico,
a taxicab rolls by the men. They shout, "Stop!"
The taxi takes the jovial crew to a Mexican
caravansary,
a house of rest from the cares of the world.
Pedro swears this whorehouse the best around.
The rates are lower in the middle day; the
American soldiers come at night.

In the corner of a huge room girls sit
knitting, crocheting bedspreads and tablecloths
of intricate designs that remind Guy of the
delicate forms Aunt Sally knit.

"What are they doing here?"—Pedro tells Guy,
"These girls, they make their dowry, then go
home to marry. A girl gotta have linen

and blankets ... these girls work hard to marry."
Red tequila hot in his queasy gut
and this domestic scene whirl in his head: five
madonnas without child sit by the wall. Then the
youngest drops her work to blandish him. Youth
to youth, she seeks his innocence, but Guy has
not found his liquor courage yet and lets this
sparrow from the desert sing to the next
customer, who buys her wings.

Three ladies put their hands upon his thigh,
tequila glows, their beauty grows, and Guy.
Alluring, accomplished, voluptuous,
a lady leads Guy to a room and tells him
to undress ... Guy watches from corner eye ...
as she reveals delightful buttocks, breasts, and
navel above a black brush of wires that shine
invitingly between her thighs. Her lips are ruby
... it's not lipstick
... it doesn't come of when she begins
to assault him ... below the belt ... she works with
professional grace ... now Dallas fades ...

O lips and breasts attacking, what were you paid
today ... testing ... Guy finds the past alive
and demands a more conventional love to save a
memory that nothing gave.

Reel IV: No Angels There

Next night the crew stops at a place where dirt
and sawdust fight for mastery of the floor, the
sheets, and every piece of furniture.
But a dollar a night sweeps linen clean and they
do not care for tables and chairs.

Neon signs complement the decor
for the traveler ... heigh ho the
wind
without rain blows tumbleweeds up the street
by Jose's Bar and Grill, by a U-Haul It to the
porno thriller on the corner. Up, up, and over
the stucco buildings,

a flock of loud-mouthed white-necked ravens
fills the evening sky. Their color and their mirth
echo Guy's thoughts—fear gives them top billing
...

Here Guy is, strolling down the boulevard in
Hollywood, the glow of Sunset Strip. Nearby
Kerouac, Snyder, Ginsberg, the Beats are
hovering there about the City Lights. They do
not exist for Guy, those poets, though he has
heard the Word of Ferlinghetti. Their howls
mean little to him now—
he knows Joe Page and Joe Dimaggio and roots
for their rivals every day.

The motley birds that move along the street
amaze him with their half-dressed variety.
Gauche, garish, flitting in the sun or lights from
neon signs, these moths and butterflies must
flutter, flail, flame up for poets' eyes.

Right around the corner from Grauman's
Chinese Theater the crew sets up house in an
efficiency apartment, up high. Danny gets one
sofa, Guy gets the other. Steve and Lew share
the comfort of a bed. Karl looks for quarters to
express himself next to a quiet bar for afternoon
drinks.
That's where he meets Lee come from dancing
school who leaps the tables with her lithesome
pals until six o'clock, when she dons a skirt
and serves refreshments to her able friends in
the Rooster Lounge at the happy hour.
The birds of the bar sing early and late,
they preen, coo, dance, and after hours, mate.

Odd birds sample ... Evan bums at Malibu,
spends his weekends with his wife on cheap
drunks. They go down to the beach, light a fire,
eat, drink, until they've numbed their pain ...
then, if they're able, they go to sex until they've
numbed their pain again. He doesn't pass out
toothpaste very fast and his first week on the
pavement is his last ...

George stays longer. He is a future star, affected
ass hiding behind the glass of his shades he
adjusts a bit ajar.
George regales Guy with tales of Hollywood and
has him primed for Jerry Lewis
when he bounces across the street that day as
they set out to sample the suburbs.

The Hollywood Hills solace Guy's Sundays.
Hiking up the street for several blocks
he reaches brush of the watered ravines and the
arid hills that cover their domes with leafless
scrub. Alone, he sits and stares across the
unlovely horizon-smoke
and odd mixtures of every architecture
imaginable to man. Western Pewees, Blue-gray
Gnatcatchers, Plain Titmice, bluebirds decorate
the hills with colorful wings that waft him two
thousand miles in a glance
of recognition. Days without sample paste
restore his sanity—blooms flit the breeze
slipping away from disappointing bees.

Reel V: San Diego

A roost away from home for sailors, Alice's
offers accommodations to visitors from many
nations.

On weekdays when the fleet's at sea her rooms
rent for two bucks a day. Comfortable beds
would give a good night's sleep except for
phones that ring throughout the night-desperate
groans seek the girls who give them comfort ...
"Where's Cora?"
"How can I get in touch with Terry Bird?" At
two o'clock in the morning dark Guy finds it
difficult to understand their need. Sailors have
his curse, curt, unkind to this comedy of quails.
Down at the piers he watches shags, the
cormorants in line
on piles, fishy sailors, comic fliers. Guy works
houses in San Diego light to offers toothpaste to
ladies of the night. In their jovial mid-day
dishabille, raucous magpies greet Guy laughing
loud and asking what they can do for him
— this sample will taste good in their mouths,
"We need clean mouths in our line of work,
come on in and spend some time. We've lots of
time now. We'll show you a good time today
with the sweet-smelling breath your sample
gives"—

the dry air blows through the palms, and he
dreams that gentle female fingers touch his hair
... laughter rudely wrecks these fragile
daydreams ... he awakes to houris' obscene
gesturing.

Hummingbirds suckle November flowers
flaming red along the rocky paths
that overlook the bay. Anna's hummingbirds'
streak about to match the flowers with their
throats.

Guy sees them on weekends of, but weekdays he
hikes the streets to pass out toothpaste and
watches flashing

wings before his face. Tri-colored blackbirds
whistle from the reeds, a mountain plover flies
across the hills, a white pelican, stately, soars on
past while Guy, earthbound, carries his sample
box from yard to yard. Beneath an evergreen he
sees a gigantic sparrow singing:
a golden-crown adorns his plodding day.

Fierce beauties, white-tailed kites surprise Guy—
you don't expect to find them in the suburbs— a
California thrasher chortles, loud, and scarlet
finches flutter in the shrubs.
Like the Pied Piper, Guy marches down the
streets of San Diego followed by little kids
who yell at him for more toothpaste, "It's good,
just like candy, good to eat." They laugh against
the toothpaste world of P & G.

Their toothy smiles of glee brighten his day. The
blue sky's loveliness increases warmth within
the heart. He wishes for a time to be back in the
joyous days of youth
...
heaven paved with terra cotta toothpaste. The
sun of southern California moves
the mind of an Easterner—Guy misses trees but
revels in the warmth he walks for fee. Ash-
throated Flycatchers yell raspingly ... they, like
the phoebes, express a harsh delight.
Steady glow, the autumn sun exposes negatives
inside Guy's throbbing skull
where reel follows reel follows reel ... rewind ...
and the motion picture show grinds on.

He attempts a flight with warblers heading
south, but momentary slips from the movie
show him that this strategy won't carry him back
to old Virginny halfway young enough to forget
what happened.

VI: Heading East

After a long climb the crew rides the peaks of
the Sierra Mountains. Winter sun
shines on the jagged rocks ... blue, red, black
hues thrust in stark lines but where brush
shields the sun.

n this brilliance Guy sees Townsend's solitaire
flying-an elegant jewel flare.

On the way east they work a week in Tucson, a
week Guy's mind careens across-crazily.
He rooms with Russ and Steve ... they see him
slip ... he hikes each day and hands out lots of
paste. Guy pushes toothpaste as if it's going out,
not in. Damn, P & G will hate to lose him. Guy
hikes to the desert for weekend excitement,
separation from the paste. The desert soothes
his heaving breast with silky flycatchers—
Phainopeplas—Inca Doves, and claws of a
goshawk set in a rabbit to end his flight.
Aiheeee! Brothers! He shouts as he senses
kinship to them both— blue sky, blue sky,
finality calms him.

Ferruginous hawks sit on saguaro trees beside
Route 66 and hover
in the sky above. Their ruddy fierceness
sends thrills along Guy's neck ... he longs to soar
with them, but still he runs too fast in thought to
feel easy with their circling symmetry. The
Aplamado Falcon pleases him
more because the swift flight on steadfast line
promises an escape from repetition. Swimming
eagerly in the blue he pours his strength into
attack's severity—

rare, taloned bird, Guy wishes flight with you
to shake the grimy dust from of his mind— but
there, you fly, and he is left behind.

As they move into Colorado Rockies the forests
rise about them and the snow lies thick upon the
ground. Forced to stop for traffic stuck in mush,
they clamber out.
Gray-headed juncos fly among the trees, russet
backs sparkle against green and white
to brighten landscape ... solitaires and snowbirds
make irregular yet certain flight to art.
Guy's mind glows with the scenery he sees at
day and night ... kaleidoscopes press him on
though pain inhibits thoughtfulness.

O for a life of sensation, surreal
color, rather than cold sweats in the dark. If only
he could frame his mind with birds to soar
beyond the summer scenes that rush upon him
... if wings or art can conquer he may escape the
woven plot he fears—

He remembers the lark bunting black and white
beside his small brown mate flitting the sage—
orange, blue, against the purple mountain range
in morning sun ... the sky is eggshell blue ... the
sun warms the artisan, unpolluted.

The picture show across Guy's mind rolls on,
reel after reel flashes frames Guy cannot stop.
As the train sways on through coastal Delaware
shadows from yellow lights and high, dark spires
cast Dantesque shapes over Chesapeake Bay,
match chimaeras within his whirling brain that
lurch over the tracks of sanity—
he can never reach home again with ease.

Norfolk is a few hundred miles away by railroad
car, but he runs in the West.

His late show offers him no intermission.
In the dim lights around the wharves gulls hover
and cry ... if he had their wings he'd fly...
in the end, his movie is too real for Guy.

Historical Places and Perspectives

Urbania

This whore of a modern world
has high, firm nipples of concrete blocks and
brittle hair of steel that's curled
with the rhythmic sway of hammer shocks.
Under us she lies in her false heat
And gives us a half-hearted kiss whose acrid
taste exudes deceit and mocks our urbane
synthesis.
We moderns love this skilled professional and
buy her on seductive city streets;
her SUV's, stock quotes, and other pals
we crave as addicts crave their killing treats.
Yet we fear her price is growing high
and sense that something's badly gone awry.

Subway Rites

People crowd the underground to move under
city streets an unnatural way. Mole-like they
travel tunnels in a groove

at speeds that might a grubbing mole dismay.
This action does not make an easy play for genial
spirits or for humane talk.

Every day their skies are gray and riders sigh
and many wish that they could sometimes walk
instead of riding subways passing by. Elbow into
rib, foot on other's foot they beg a pardon and
justify flattened arches as the price they pay to
root out the hatred as they hide the impact
in friendly gestures, acts to stay disputes.

Mound Builders

Here, where too many of my friends have
stopped to leave their gifts of waste I thrust
among their colorful bins to find odd artifacts to
suit my taste.

I watch as fragile leaves blanket the rubbish—
technology to which we have entrusted
our lives to create ease and instant bliss forged
in garish forms inviting dust.

Plastic bottles gain brief permanence, a value
littering our design.
Their age betrays our best sense and rusts the
edges of our minds.

Less brittle than a falling leaf
these modern forms smart men have made of
plastic, glass, and metal. I feel grief' at their
longevity, for which we've paid.

Black Mountain: 1930

A man stood caged in his hell And watched the
angry files go by.
Jesse watched the walls of his cell And heard the
buzz of bloating flies.

Some said Jesse boy meant rape. He didn't have
an eye for money. "Oh yeah, old Jesse can't
escape now. We've paid his lawyer's fee."

Late one night men visited jail And dragged
Jesse out to their cars. Up at the Gap Jesse
looked pale When he dangled under the stars.

Georgia Southern in Norfolk, 1950

On the street, the lights blink GAIETY! Inside
the front, bare on a stage Bump meets grind in a
grin For ecstatic animals she's caged.
The burlesque dancer warms her men And other
admiring friends.
She calls to them, quivering, splits, Swings her
mass and twitches a hip Bringing hands deftly
past her crotch To make a smacking sound of

meat hit Stripped on svelte loins in motion, hot.
Pounding drums and wriggling pelvis Fire eyes with desire for a kiss
When contortion lifts the light gauze Mocking her viewers' distant paws
As they imagine what they've missed.. Down on one knee, slim leg stretched round, Ogling gaze with movements for thinkers,
Sighs, gives together breast pounds And offers body- stretch glimmers Of the parts she has danced around. Outside, the street lights blink GAIETY!

Recessional

When a dark night comes, shadows disappear into their element except where lights echoing sunshine bring out chimeras
for those who walk streets under city lights. In the morning, sun draws forth true shadows on the streets to stir up candy rainbow wrappers. Back and forth aimlessly they float over the skulls lying on the gutter sheets, over the hands outstretched for a groat,
over the dung of the dogs that stroll for treats. Rapid walkers hurry by day's retinue as if blind to a complicity they rue.

Jamestown, 1958

Mosquitoes still sting
In summer places
On the same surface
Of malarial water
Giving no quarter
Producing larvae
That swelled the fevers
In the gentlemen
Who gazed upon
The earlier suns
Of earth's only paradise
Whose later bites give stings
That only worry
People in a hurry.
Now a curio store
Sits on the land
Where many starved
While sitting on their backsides
With fevered pride
Instead of turning a hand
To the hoeing of corn.

Opposable Thumbs

As grail or phoenix feather whirls in air
Promethean hero grasps it there, audacity for immortality
rends upper air to prove man free.

Fired beyond his slime toward the sun, he
counts stanchions blessings run through
implemented mammal hairs grace astronaut with
palms at prayer.

Caesar's Head, S. C., 1960

American primitive,
old Indian,
he stands out watching
swallows chasing flies
in roller-coaster snatches,
summer wings
obsidian in skies
where leathery things
had flown eons

before totems touched the sky to signify man's
bond with earthy core.
Still swallows fly
about his face
as new savages defy
wonder drenched in red
to grace
a wind-hewn Phidian.

Dragstrip

Concrete straight-aways on our highways
challenge us to rapid races in the sun, not only
why and where, but how we run while rubber
tires squeal loudly as we play. Even though we
build mighty raceways for soul-enticing motor
motions
with faster speeds to satisfy fond notions, the
screech of tires that tests attempts at tracing
mileage markers along our days
with nuts and bolts and rods wears us away.
Racing mind and body all life long
can cause desire to brake and restart to blend
with a daft mechanic's song to justify the racing
human heart.

At Arlington, 1965

Over these three tombs that mark the dead The
marble columns rise up clean and high Above
the trees that tower the Potomac's Water blue
and placid but for boats Careening here and
there in heat,
Their wakes dividing blue with white To match
the ivory columns.

Quiet has come to their world.

In shade they lie no longer shy of death

Who took the hemlock bomb and mortar shell
To die so fast and easily. In death
They offers no regrets. The three are mute But
do not dwell in silence as the hosts, Polite and
careful, to throngs of visitors, Multitudes who
murmur at the dead.
Quiet has come to their world.

Better that they are not known,
Not knowing, their oblivion sits high Above the
Capitol. Their classic stoicism Maintained
without the limits of a name
Honors corpses. Unknown they are immortal
And disdainful of the cameras
That click the changing of the guard.
Quiet has come to their world.

Myths for Space

The men who search toward the distant stars
will think always of home in Akron Heights. To
them their flight will seem a search for sights
more right for thrilling men than Roman Mars.

Yet space alone can breed no Greek centaurs
and men who fly on earthy emptiness
will fail to fill the void they seek to bless with
struggles taken Titan to the stars.

Dateline D. C., Prime Time: March 9, 1977

Blood flows on the carpet from wall to wall up
seven stories and on ground level painting the
citadels of men and God with crimson on green
rugs
to order up an ambulance and pall
in the name of Allah as they create hell riding
out of ghetto deserts in squads on U-Haul It
trucks as thugs

from Hamass shout Mohammed's jihad that
sweeps the streets of the Capitol clean for killers
holed up with sad hostages heads tumbled out
dark windows— jettisoned women and children
deemed bad drowned in basins, drowned in tubs
at the scene of death in the night whose strife
engages the prophet who spurns his foes

and brings Wallace Mohammed to town to talk.
Gurus of guilt say our society breeds violence
with aid from radio, TV, and newspaper
sensations
that egg on the angry hunters who stalk down
prayers despite cries Islam supersedes revenge,
demands forgiveness' embassy to unite a sick
nation.

Honking horns of morning sun celebrate the
unceremonious end of a show that filled our
void with TV vigil
the politically correct way.
ABC, CBS, NBC rate
this occasion with a corporate glow, "Did a
prophet ride today from the kill at his ghetto
hideaway?"

Lowell Seminar, 1978

Enough for the sweet-tooth bear to desecrate-
Tis open book ... my open coon.

Without a hint of guilt they break the comb, tear
the other, black claws attack—the hive of bees
unloosed about their heads annoy but do not
halt the rending paws at home with honey, the
sweet and sticky bribe
to ease the stings stuck through their furry
hides. Their nectared tongues, their colder noses
toy with the circled wax the bee has coned.

Old Lowell, you serve table for thirteen bears
with the tougher wax that dark bees make.
Ambivalent, like flowers, you court
the tearing hands of hungry, growling bears.
Your sugar waits the honey guide who wakes
those bears to smash your coffin for their sport.

Dream Trip

I fell asleep over Egyptian lore
and marveled at strange lands. Spirits rowed the
boat I traveled in among the stars
and drew me past heavenly sand bars and fields
of wheat
fire-shod like pharaoh on a golden barge the
ghostly rowed
to fallow fields under white-hot suns. The
rowers lifted and dipped their oars in shadow-
stroking unison to send my soul to join scores
who sought Osiris on the brighter Nile

where the sky-high earth awaits grain sowed by
ushebtis on miles and miles of starlit land
covered in cane
upturned by oxened plows on a demesne
beyond the Water Lily Lake
where Anubis measures men's mistakes.
My judgment day still waited when I waked.

Triassics

At the beginning of an age The awakening actors
Crowded onto a bloodstained stage.
Small, bright
Eyes sparkled
In the ancient forest night.

Lemurs and tarsiers raised their hands
Successively, aggressively,
And debated
The fate
Of the world with their opposable thumbs
While huge reptilian bodies Crashed around them Futilely.
The shrews spoke, too,
But the vote was called
In favor of the brainy mites And they,
As did the Vedic Krishna In a later day
(when he spoke of courage and duty to Arjuna)
In the times of volcanic terror And fires
Exhorted their followers
To victory
Upon the steppes
And plains,
In the jungles of Africa and Asia. I wonder that great Krishna
Had in mind We are all
Products of fratricide.

Totentanz

Museum skeletons recall my dream
of sauroids swimming that calm stretch of ocean
called Sargasso Sea.

They bowed their necks in question marks with rhythmic grace as they swam in unison to land.

Swimming to the beach
they crawled awhile away from ocean
before they left their bones in muddy streams:

Those swimmers now are dead though we walk on erected
to note their drowning on the land we tread.

Primal Question

Was there ever foolish man named Adam,
reluctant wearer of a fig-leaf cover? Did he bug out of Eden on the lam
or was he myth of some burnt Hebrew lover?

Modern Technology

Pleistocene bears and lions roamed Europe and disputed the rule of the land with mammoths and Mousterian man
who huddled in the bear's old cave and cupped his ears to hear the roars echoed the hills.
He dreamed of daylight and the coming kill. In the light of day growls frighten less
as he fingers the bear's teeth that will bless the plan of a stone-and-muscle engineer

whose technology will slay the giant bear or marauding lion whose mane he prizes. The fears he feels he hides for he despises men who throw their weapons down and run. The rule of technical man had just begun.

Embarkation

Jellyfish and trilobites flowed free
in water womb while Icthyostega bore his bulk
to bleak and cold expanses whose psilophytes
urged roaming more.

Out from watery edge, therapsid tree turned
double eyes on terra firma shore whose moon
and star and planet dances beckoned them to
roam some ages more.

Up from Devonian coasts, we stand free with
mind on past and future shore. Inherited
primate curiosity prompts us to lift ourselves
with rocket's roar.

Paleolithic Ax

The form inheres in the stone where the poet
seeks its shape by flakes with which he can hone
from rock the poetry of blade.

Children of Daedalus

Hut gave way to palace and pyramidal grace and
the donjon keep
to skyscrapers that leap
to clouds in a concrete race.

Carefully worked stones followed implementary
bones that gave way to swords forged for
tyranincal lords.
We have not lost our urge to hone.

Old Architects

The ziggurat towered bricks
of Sumer, Chaldea, and Babylonia betray the
waste to our newer tricks although we're
somewhat stonier.

Because he dared the priests of Bel-Marduk Old
Nabonidus lost his empire to the conquering
Persian fire. He spent his time digging for record
books.

His searches conferred no success to
Belshazzar's army, poorly led and unprepared,
falling defeated before the swords of Cyrus'
conquest.

Despite Nabonidus' time at play while his
empire burned, his ancestors had learned
to build substantially with clay.

Had he paid heed to the lessons of those who
had created bricks he might have known to rely
on their
clever architectural tricks.

Jilted

Dido mourns and thinks of his caresses
enthralled with his touch even on her pyre and
echoing his shape in leaping fire
as the flames eat flesh he still possesses while
she thinks of Trojan sails in the breeze and finds
no memories that can appease the tragic mask
she wears in the light
of his deceit. She sings her last song tonight.
With a nod to the gods, Aeneas' love sails of to
destiny. Her anguish sings
across the waves to blend with cheers that ring
from the throats of his sailors who shove their
oars into the sea.
The woman sings to the flames of her banquet's
fiery love.

Thanet Isle, 449 A.D.

The blow fell, the empire broke asunder;
horsemen and hunters pushed on weakened
Rome luring the leathered legions homeward.
They left a half-tamed land to melted men,
people untaught of spears, unable to sing the
ancient Celtic lays of race-birth.
Then, over the wrath of northern oceans out of
fjords and coves came bold seafarers: Hengist's
men looked at their haggard shores and longed
for the rolling British hills.
In their boredom they recalled chalky cliffs
as mead cups lay drained in mead-numbed
hands and the bard's harp strumming raised no
head to listen as he sang of Scylding's deeds.
They sobered, then gave rise to bloody plans
that set the dragon ships upon the sea.

Anthropology Lecture

"Students," proclaimed the careful pedagogue,
"no doubt you've heard of Arthur Pendragon,
who for many centuries has set the world agog.
For hundreds of years he's raised his flagon in
gilded, unduly romantic stories. In fact," the
professor paused for emphasis, "the literature is
full of him and his ploys and how his knights
heroically defeated lists

of evil men and ogres who deflowered and
devoured British maidens in their lust for power.
In all the lands of fabled lore
there is no king like Arthur, none is spoke of
more, or lied of more convincingly,
but the truth of the matter seems to be his
sword,
Excalibur, wore gaudy bands
of polished Roman iron, and the wielder's father
had been a little loathe to see the Roman legions
head for Gaul and the Imperial power.
So, there you see him, a hand-me-down
swordsman with a deep-gorged brow to stand
upon a barreled ton of sensual flesh;

the noble Guinevere was a camp-girl fresh
from the fields who loathed her brutish
husband's drunken ways and daily dallied on the
side with that
smoothie, Lancelot. She cried
when she thought of that lump, her husband.
Knowing this, how can we speak of Camelot as a
misty, storied place without a blot
on maidens who took their troubles there.
Arthur met the Saxon, not in stoic calm But in a
liquored passion
fired by the balm of gold his fellow Britons paid
for care. Artoriosus, Bear, was what a querulous
monk called him. Bear struck terror in his foes

because of massive limbs and strength—a hunk
to solve some sluttish British maiden's woes. He
dwells in romance now, not history, the glow
that fabled lore can spin around a hulking brute.
Marvelous tales are told of how he strove to
amaze men with greatness of repute
in a world where evil men were rendered mute.
Ladies and gentlemen, we scholars know
his heroic struggles were self-centered, not the
noble acts admiring poets entered in tales of
Lancelot in Celtic lore."

Dead Scholarship

On travel posters from the past and in the
newsreels now and then tall, vine-covered
Angkhor Vat threw shadows with a solemn cast,
spread broken temples in the sun and threw
down pagoda patterns shining from reflective
pools lying placidly and quietly dun beside hoof-
marks in trampled burns where the shouting
peasants and their water buffaloes' feet
have churned Cambodian jungle ferns— at least
until a red star rose

insisting scholars march their feet to bony fields
of red deceit to supersede the buffaloes.

Yeats' Statues: a Commentary

Pythagoras gave the Grecians factors
To make the hair, the lips, the eyes to move By
numbers wrought in marble character,
Lost on all but boys and girls in love
Who dreamed a fleshly statue's grace could act
to hold the love they feared an artifact.
They pressed at midnight in a public place Live
lips upon a plummet-measured face.

So they grew to sensuous godhead, the youths
That believed a chiselled stone or frieze
That looked like actual flesh could stem the
truth Of oars upon the Hellespont, that these
Emboldened numbers wrapped in rock could
drown The million oars of Salamis with stone,
That imagined sense could defeat harsh sounds
With ideals made manifest in sculpted bone.

Image of flesh wounded abstraction's cage
But marched to an Indic tree where it grew fat
And lost humanity. Victim of hydra rage,
Conqueror was conquered. Icon sat
Inhuman and gazed with no urge to know The
wisdom of unreal and pulsing number, Avoided
sight of eyeballs that enjoy a show: Empty eyes
found meaning in self-slumber.

When Yeats summoned Cuichulain to his aid He
did not call him from the eastern land Where
Gautama sat blank and unamazed.
Yeats called him forth from olive groves at hand,
From Irish Greece where modern heroes stride
Upon the ground that Celtic blood has dyed.
Yeats searched for symbols there that he might
trace Live lips upon a plummet-measured face.

Intelligent Designer

From out of a whirlwind thundered epithets:
"Do not blame God for pious blasphemies
uttered by proud fellows, My failed prophets.
God tolerates messengers such as these who
think He cannot work divine mysteries that
evolve as men's comprehension lets them realize
their Lord's complexities.
My words are worked awry by false prophets. It
is not easy for proud men to see
as cousins those who grin like chimpanzees or
those who create bowers like fishnets. I'm the
nine hundred pound gorilla, right?" Trembling, I
answered despite my fright, "I believe in God
the Father Almighty and in Christ, His only
begotten Son."
The thunderous voice replied, "It is your right to
doubt those who preach rigid religion
proclaiming nature's God implicitly

gives them the wisdom to eliminate the
changing concepts of evolution and
circumscribe mysterious origins
by denying ancient life while preaching hate. Do
you rule God? Do they? What rash men puffed
up with pride set limits to their maker? Did they
create a universal order?
It that first thought about God became man,
Why carp on what flesh came before Adam?"

Surreal Songs

The Maker

The poet must dip into his soul
(or what Freud terms the Id) to dredge out
mysteries that lie in wait for their parole
from jail of nerves whose crooked circuits flout
the self: to look, ask, force words to resemble
emotions that show red impress
of human flesh in both silk and burlap dress,
emotion taut and not dissembled.

Humanity revealed is half the fight
for freedom of the thoughts he truly feels but
must divide into artistic light
and depth and form: his consciousness congeals
a clot of words to stop the flow of thought
from passing back into the shadow world—
caught by making word curl about idea to wheel
forever symbol, forever wrought.

Kinetics

No marabou for us
who do not care to understand why the devil fell
to dust or that we sit on earthy land halfway
between chaos and hell where artifacts made to
sell satisfy no man who will not curse a
providential hearse. Still, we count to three

to seek divinity,
but find perfected actions in chain reactions, at
blinking bar ways
and neon copulations,
our sins revealed by scientific play in a tube of
DNA.

Hedonist at the Madhouse

Pour qui sont ces serpents
Qui sifflent sur vos tetes?
Andromache (mad)

Les liocephalles, pal, lizards, not snakes.
Crawl down to the pit (quit), live with your
friends from San Francisco, the brave young
poets who strive (thrive)
just to stay alive on dope.
They see hipsters.

Hipsters witched my brother. See that wiggle?
That dance. A trance. That's what they put my
friend (covered in soot) into. Who? The young
man who (to rue) chinned himself on the tavern
bar (his star that guided him after lights out).

Poets have the favors of that doll there.
What's her name? What is that dame's name?
Circe?

You bet, brother, no other broad's that game.
Circe, yes, the temptress, like no other
Girl who ever owned an island (don't pout
About it man, she'll do another dance.
Her real name's Helen, see that abortion scar?)
She makes those poets sing (fling out) their
song:

> We live on jimson weed,
> It cures our insatiable need,
> My brother bore a stalk about;
> You don't need to rant, just shout
> Your tale told by your sweet mother.
> We are not idiots, we're just hooked, brother.

That was a batch of bull, here, have a drink.
Their tale is full of heartache. On life they flake.
You know, it was laughter at it (Attic)

That gave Greek gods (those odds) the
bellyache. Maudlin poets ('Terpe's pets) are not
tragic.

Killing Time

Our cards are played with little care. The lights
that strike us on the run from solitaire to soaking
up the sun hint an instrumentalist of air
has missed a cue or muffed a pitch somewhere.
The lights
of red and blue and white that splay our roaming
holiday
give us fright of pause
and warn us to find cause
we pirouette in flickering stars declaring
instrumentalist of air
has missed his cue or muffed a pitch somewhere.
To forget our internal wars,
we play another game of solitaire.

49er: De Gustibus ...

He wishes for shade, not shots of sun imbibed
By the tall, sad saguaros resigned
To standing mute on parched and rocky earth.
A lean and naked arm gives little birth
To water under pebbles scraped away
As it digs underneath a river baked to clay.
Rocks sparkle like gold in c offers box.

Oh my darlin' Clementine's gold locks..
Imagined drunkenness of rocks and sand
Mockingly defies a scratching man.
Sensitive fingers sense their act's undone
By rocks sarcastically aimed at the tongue
Some god has swollen to grate upon a cheek
To curse inscraping hand along dry creek.
Rocks rattle underneath a creosote bush. Oh my
darlin' Clementine's warm kiss.

Sails and Indigo ...

lips carry heavy cargo of bunting and indigo
schemes, in touch of deep blue on skin's pink
cockatoo
for the neap envelopment of those thoughts
present on sand under the bend of the knee and
the wavy force of the sea.

Flambeau ...

glowing sun-red ships sailing with cargo to
leeward,
to Sunday dresses galing on slim-waisted girls
tarred by
the storm clouds cowling close over the
schooner charred
by my love's hair trailing
in the wind's force, fiery, starred.

Road Race

We are the lads of little deaths in love with a girl
named Thrill who funds our motors' auto
breaths and races us over the hills.

We think her sporty car a van
to move us fast from morning's sack.
We flee another seductive scan on her maniacal
rack.

We slip into our curves beset by our girl with
mechanic guile who smiles and flicks a cigarette
as we drive into the night in style.

Liftoff for Mars

Not knowing why, they placed me on the pad
while moving stars proclaimed nativity
beyond their lovers' dreams whose lives lacked
space.

After the countdown came, the rockets flamed:
screaming, into the clouds I soared at ease,
unseen the cords that held me to the ground.

Nine months with stay-connected rope umbilical
brought blast to push me forth with jets
programmed for murder myths.

War Games

Armored column speeding hard,
Parsifal thunders to heel
Now dismaying castle guards
In fear of clanking wheels.

Parsifal's howitzers clamor
Against castle walls redoubt.
Their music plays with candor,
No chivalric peel or shout.

Bold, destructive guns subdue,
Shouts heartless steel. Those inside
Quake. Heavy metallic blue
Threatens with a clanging stride.

Castle bridge rolls down to cold
Steel tracks. Parsifal falters
On beleaguered stony threshold,
By Molotov cocktail altered.

It's A Jungle Out There

A rajah omnipotence sways splendid
Indian elephants guiding his intended
Through a monkey jungle alive with howls,
Owl calls, tiger screams, frogmouth growls
That break the sleep of Maharanee's night.

Nightjars and thrush jays duet in moonlight
Emitting liquid sounds that soothe her.
Languidly the princess' musicians stir
Their strings. Their rhythms embody craft
As they sound through monkey jungle miles
Whose animals hunt while deadly arrows whir
A vengeful ire on gleaming yellow shafts.
Under sunlit skies, unheeding guile,
Swimmers stir the jaws of lounging crocodiles.

Trips

The druggings of our inconstancy
lead mixed-in-acid brains
from the squeals of infancy
to the tracks of insane trains.

We desire a colorful ride
while traveling all our world
and gathering wealth besides
before the last train has whirled

its demanding, mocking wheels
to the heated invections
and insidious peals
of destiny's drugged directions.

Man's Buddy

In our feed bin sits a defiant rat

who curses the claws of our barnyard cats, eats
his fill of grain and grows rather fat—
a magician of meanness and rabies spit with
ability to give us shivers lit
in the redness of his eyes, narrow slits that leer
with evil, apocalyptic glow
of small brain cunning that lets us know here is
an animal who has seen the low side of the
universe and that those teeth,
which chew down on corn in pouches, give
sheath of muscles a cutting strength, a wreath
of sharp death that has played with flesh as well
as eaten the fat grain fresh
in the trough or left where the chickens thresh.
Snarling, murderous magic of rat
sits on his haunches and shows us that he's not
afraid of man's god damn cats.

Sharing

When a wandering hero
asks hurt men to sing their woe they cause his
eager ears
to ring unpleasantly no doubt,
for they quite loudly shout that he must share
their stings.

Sans Sense

The Buddha's rhinos walk alone.

Their master has taught them to cut
Emotion's excess to the bone,
Good disciples almost brute.
They seek to reach a senseless state
By thrusting of their sensuous foes.
What sorrows do they see await
Bold men that shun cold placebos?

Useful Catbriar

Uncle Remus termed a briar patch the downy
nest where ineffectual pests,
droll and clever,
elude deep scratches
with animal endeavor.

Luther wrote, "Es gibt ein Fehler" and posted his
99 articles offering impolitic particles of truth
for paler souls who didn't know how high a devil
to defy.

Should we appreciate a friend who pushes us to
a thornier
contemplation of the path's end by using
bramble bushes around the corner?

Cold Tracks

On tracks of limbo fled my mind
Along the railways of the brain

Where all the stations on the line
Stood dark to my locomotives.

Images of train and track lit
All my dreams. They would invade
My sleep, but they could never fit
In. My mind refused its function.

So I sent engines out to junctions
Far beyond grim railways inspired
By my engineer. His conjunctions
Were too bleak for me. I had him fired.

Lessons Unlearned

Plato's apostles
go importunate lengths
to set our brains ajostle
with eternal drinks
that offers unseen
the bright ideals
always demeaned
because men feel.

Family Tree

Is it a mortal sin
To deny a cousin?
We love mysteries
And learned arguments

About the number three.
Who would deem it evident
Young Eohippus gallops
In the best of beds
And chimpanzees
Easily learn to chase
Slender Jane Goodall
Around a jungle tree
To pick her fleas
While filling their stomachs
With store-bought bananas,
Or, impulsively,
Deign to eat meat
Tearing flesh from the bone,
Smacking wide lips,
Then belching politely
An oriental primate contentment While sipping their tea?
Now we must say That ninety per cent Or more of our DNA Claims much ancient Evidence of family descent.

Deer Sighting

From flowered roadside a startled doe sprang through the green yard, ran into the house hide.
The flaming red sign

of her head arched high seared my tinder mind
with running wildfire. Road kills are turned in,
not legally kept.
When their fires burn men they waste heart's
unrest.

Idealists ...

Like weeds cut for the sap to run,
our hopes fall down at a thrusting scythe
whetting their crowns from stalks that writhe
while thoughts shout; one or two snickers mark
the ended bouts waged with cankers.

Urban Olympics

"I didn't like the way he rapped and jived, but he
looked Olympian in that dive." Just like a pal at
ease, he grabbed my arm And caught my eyes
and my shrinking alarm. I thought him one of
the bums from the park
Whose bottles crawl with bugs and gutter garp.
"My buddy jumped of that building, up there.
Like a skydiver, he flew a minute
At least. He used no prayer or parachute. He
floated for a moment in the air
without a cord or silk. He was astute. It was a
hoot. Another day I'll try Olympic air...."
I nudged aside a ragged man's despair, Fearful of
his eagerness to gain repute.

A Final Solution?

In days far past recall of us
who wander down the modern maze some men
of Greece once wandered thus while Buddha sat
in seery daze, but sages waking now will die
to leave their questions in their stead;
like other searchers long gone by
the Buddha and the Greeks have fled.

We wonder why they sought to cease; we sigh at
them but think we shall uncover truth. To plead
a lease
on life adds zest to our morale, but Hamlet's
qualms at suicide no longer teach us to abide.

Dental Evolution

Tigers among us bare great saber teeth dripping
glowing blood and growing longer as they slice
up dovish prey whose grief increases tigrish
appetite gone wrong.

I recall that teeth too long may shrink
From lacking meat. Empty mouths and growling
guts are what caused saber-tooths to grow
extinct when tusks grew longer than the prey
they cut.

One-way Trip

Nina, dear, sign up for a trip to the moon.
It's all the rage. We're leaving soon.
What's a million or so of earthly gain?

I wonder. Do you choose your captain?
If he's a hunk, it might be worth the money.

Nina, we mustn't bother how he looks, honey.
Women our age don't complain like a whore.
You must abandon complaint. It's a bore.
Like an old corset, it's too luxurious to be funny.
Times have changed for lack of space. Our times anoint
A society out of joint with our stars. That's a point Poets have pummeled for centuries
Of fire and ice, but now it's our disease.
Spacemen have nothing on that cow who leaped
So high she circled her neighbor's sphere and reaped For mankind condensed milk in our coffee cups And dime store gadgets and satellite pups.

Let's go. In space ships we'll limp with creaking joints To our final dim, uncharted point.

Old Wives' Tales

Ghosts come at odd hours to haunt men the old
crones used to tell the children; but ghosts are
not always confined to haunting hours assigned:
we march through shadow days; content to hide
from our dark nights, we erect electric
monuments
to drive away the witching time's suspense with
incandescent lights.
We cringe beneath a hardened shell
of toughened flesh enveloping old fears of
witches tending flames to sear
our shadow world with chants of hell.
We are like locusts grubbing in the earth
who seek to cast of a chitinous shell
yet cannot climb to sun to find new birth;
our hidden fears we cannot admit to our
neighbors' prying glances; ambiguously blessed,
we move our spirits round and round in an
internal dance.

Campfire

Burnt by the sun the savages sit to eat
Around their fiery circle's leaping glee
Upcasting shadows over sand and sea
And canines lurking to devour a bony treat:

The men and women squat to gnaw their meat.
Their raucous laughs and primal grunts declare
This beachfront campfire is an old affair
And glowing embers underscore their feat.
Sage squaw and willing mate will soon deceive
What ancient marriage rites thought to relieve.
With fierce fun lustful glares they pair
To seek their blankets' contraceptive care.
Their hot rites have an ancient heritage
But these savages savor a new age.

Desert Blooms

Cowboy Judas
Rides a radioactive horse
To his wrangling place,
Rides atomic hearse
From the Eden of first curse
To billowing clouds.
Shrouds cradle our sun
In a hydrogen
Annihilation.
Crucifixion and hanging
Served as archetypes.
We learn to ease our angst
With handy wipes.
We are blown away
By small children's games:
They will count before

Coming, ready or not.
Three, two, one, ZERO.
The ground is getting hot.
One, two, three,
Here we come infinity,
Our bid for divinity.

Ostriches

From donning synthetic satin to the factory
clang at matins,
we hide our thoughts to ease the whir of car and
cocktail pother.

Forgetfulness is bargain folly, an inexpressive
dolly on which we moderns seek to roll away
our past, and soul.

Circe's Lover

Foolish boy, why do you tremble so?
You loved me, you said, and my wine so much.
Stay here and taste my deathless love and grow
Like an immortal god. I hate to chide such
A glorious youth as you, but you must
Share my bed of lilies, my marble halls flushed
With Pompeian pink. I will not let you go.
Stay here with me and revel. Do not go
To her, to Persephone. She's cold
And has a husband too. Let my profession

Of desire, my call to frolic softly fold
Away your inconstancy and make us one
Again. I will not ever let you free
To love me less than cold Persephone.

I love you well enough, dear Circe,
But you can see I need Persephone more. My
thoughts are ever of her who thrills me
With the soft black color of her hair. Her doors
Are always open to her lover. I live no longer On
account of wanting you, sweet Circe,
For I am enthralled with a stronger Mistress, one
who will not let you delay me With your sighs. I
give you up, my mistress, As did brave Ulysses. I
leave your wine Although I love you as my life.
My empress, You must drink the liquor of
another's vine. I love your sun-kissed arms, dear
Circe,
But my drooping hands have found Persephone.

Paternity

Father hocked peace many years ago.
He waved as he marched off to fight.
He knew a price was on his foe
Just like any store-bought item.
He never came back from war to say
Litter bearers carried men from trenches.
The cost turned out to be the solemn day

They bore the hero's corpse and stenches.

The Music Contest: Retrospective

Thousands of years ago I sat down here
And played a song accompanied by thrushes;
Then young girls came to listen, shyly to peer
From banks grown still except for rushes
Swaying to the rhythm of my silver lyre,
Told with music how my worth had been maligned, Told how I, Phoebus, was moved to ire
Against deaf Midas, that humbug heretic I gave a prize of donkey ears designed To show him what he knew of music: The pipes of Pan sounded pleasing tunes, But Apollo plays mainly for Muses.
Pan made merry marches on the reeds he'd hewn, And Midas thought music only amuses.
King Midas sat down and judged a while; At last, after many a thoughtful nod
He said, "Sir, your tunes have a sort of style, But to me they sound quite strange, so odd I must disagree with Tmolus and his sneers. I, Midas, award the prize to Pan."
So Pan got palms and Midas got asses' ears,

The proper things for so dense and dull a man.
He hid them under a special cap,

Swore his barber with dark oaths to enwrap His ears in secrecy, but desire broke bounds. By this stream the barber bent and whispered, "Midas has asses' ears." The rushes heard.
They grow each spring to murmur revealing sounds.

Pilgrimage

Reborn on a psychiatric couch
from the womb of an easy-virtued shark, an optimistic Freudian sailor slouched down to sail as helmsman to a barque.

He set out seeking brave new worlds and dreaming of a tropic paradise where he could satisfy the ego hurled too often at the bias of the dice.

The eastern shores receded quickly from his modern Telemachian ship stringing lines and foam out thickly from the tiller in the searcher's grip.

Awakened after somnolent ocean days, the seeker encountered an untamed heart. He deemed his journey gone astray and voiced regrets for a misread chart.

Environmental Hues and Blues

Winter Fare

Wings hover silence as a harrier slowly seeks a
mouse or vole;
to keep his slim form from hunger some other
life must pay the toll.

The gray wings fold and talons drop
Upon the prey whose cries transform
The whitened world in bloody swap
Beyond tears, as form gives way to form.

Passion and the Desert

Full throttle
came the goshawk in his hurtle at his prey—
ten eons and ten feet away
caught sight of me,
applied wind-scuffing brakes.

He looked across man-million years of fire and
gods (I thought in fear) with fierce disdain
before he circled free and shied away from me
in search of rabbit prey.

When I turned back amid the cross-like cactus
to my coffee by the fire and my stale taunts of
god, I knew myself, a liar.

Yard Care

Whacking away
the wild things
my neighbor manicures his lawn, he is retired
and cutting weeds is something to do.
His dandelions are dug up
while mine run wild
with a mass of green and gold whose yellow
hawkeyes dance in the breeze on the spring
lawn.
His tulips and marigolds bloom only within well-
tended beds,
and any tree or brush
that defies him
by getting out of bounds invites a sharp ax. He
tends his yard,
not mine—
I desire some days
to yell at him

to let some wild things live.

Peccadilloes

In my dreamland locale there were times as a
child when I rode the hogs in glee over the
hilltops and the trees. I rode all wild in dreams
whose colors glimmered like the gleams at
sparkle in the boar hog's
small and flesh-ringed eyes. I rode red hogs and
green with black and white between;
mixed in color and flecked with mud the
brilliant hogs ran
to the naive emotion laughing at a pastel notion
that peppermint peccaries demand implicit
statements of desire.

Links

Curved wings hover escarpment rocks.
A fat rock hyrax whistles fear
of their shadow. The whistler's shock pierces the
ear.

The dark volcanic rocks embrace an eagle's nest.
Humans ask why an elephant's cousin should
race the eagle's sky.

Curiosities of nature abound in ancient Rift Valley rocks. Not all eccentric creatures ape manliness.

A Substitution

We are a picnic people on the run who stand
awhile upon the sandy cliffs and stare across the
ocean far away, watching clouds form
hieroglyphs around the punctures of the sun.

At our backs tall buildings
poke their towers high and stark above the
furious honks of motor horns which symphonize
the loves
of small and frightened worldlings.

Across the water lie the golden isles where
happy savages danced and sang about a careless
sort of life
until the apostles of steel fangs substituted cans
for coconuts and smiles.

Cumberland Gap

Hiking the forest,
in its half lights
the blinking actors recoil from the shadow sights
as they toil
with their beasts on the hoof.

They complain
about the miles they march yet disdain to ease
their act and rest tired feet in bivouac.
Led by the restless scout whose tales taunted
their beds and set them west on a heading—
stilling their doubt and fear of losing hair
from something far more savage than care
or pulling it in dotage.
They follow Boone's blaze,
their stars twinkle, then sprinkle
a geologic condiment
into the maw of stony earth,
that old crone
who spouts her excrement to build monuments
of rock embracing us all, even those who drag-
race dreams over the hag in motorcars.

Grandfather Mt. Salamander Hunt

Grandfather's Plethodon welleri encompasses
blood, rebinds the fiber once served giants of
dragonflies and beetles now encased in amber.
Where spruce and fir and yellow birch veneer
the floor, I seize moldy crud to study wriggling
amphib urchin's legs freckled with ancient mud.
With zigzagged streaks of gold and green
Weller's Plethodon casts a spell amazed the man
who found its sheen to gain its naming for death

knell when Weller's steep descent to death
footnoted salamander breath.

Homage to Ruskin Freer: Naturalist

Rose, indigo, ochre birds on Blue Ridge
peaks, maple stirrings, flowers on mountain
fields paraded in his column's friendly gaze;
imparting them to us he built a bridge to nature's
cornucopia to yield
Freer gifts when he explained its ways.
He took me out one day, spring sun ablaze. At
leafing Otter Peaks we shared afield a Lincoln's
Sparrow all too rarely seen.
In rambling woodlands, he found cause to wield
his pen to take us to the Natural Bridge
to watch kalmia and rhododendron preen their
flowers white and pink and set in green for
those who wander paths along the ridge.

Evening Movement

Traffic whizzes by row upon row of cottages
edging their boards toward the beach.
As shadows creep along the boulevard edge in
late evening appears a lonely girl
to touch the cool wind blowing from the sea
down to the brown knee of the sand.

Stooping, preening a reluctant curl, she tries to
place it as the wind frees the hair from her
clutching hand.
Jet trails etch across the darkening day as the sea
foam ripples about her feet and an oil tanker
lumbers across the bay.

The reach of sand shimmers like chrome while
her footprint in the sand retreats leaving an
undergarment of foam.

She watches the raucous tern on raid
diving for fish in the bay where pilings stand. It
glows roseate in the dropping sun.

The fisher's trade he plies from piles at parade
rising waist-high out of the sand.
The tern drops straight and rises on the run—
wise and selfish for its downy young—
from the ravening gulls; eluding maws at hand
with swift strokes he races home before the
light.

This fish will feed the craws of terns tonight
while the girl's foot arches in the touch of
twilight and she savors the salt air galing
as the water reaches upward in the night to kiss
the evening stars now trailing out their laces as
the girl seeks stasis.

Modernity

Over concrete walls dim suns may rise. All day a
busy city wrings its hands while choking the gas
of its demise in the dank streets where the
traffic stands.

Signs of life, the snow geese in their flight move
past the evening fumes in a wedge
that commends larks and jays and woodland
hikes to those gasping under concrete ledges.
Early willows give suburban's hints of life by
signaling in cyclic code as returning indigo
buntings sing
from telephone wires that ring the roads.

What armies of suburban sprawl are marching to
damn the deadly fumes at city halls?
Who heeds the hint from hawk and swallow
wing riding the winds and circling the thermals?

Prologue

The soft whir of wind postures a bend
and formal bowing from the pines on March
evenings when the small frogs peep signs of
seasonal yawning.

Farm Lands Remembered

Breezes blow up lightly in the flatlands to ease
the humid calms of summer suns, throw the red-
white tassels on fuming corn amid a rustling in
the heavy fields. Then dark clouds ride and
thunder peals.

We hear voices out in the summer crops, the
kingbird's defiance of the raiding crow, the quail
in thickets talking low together,
the meadowlark's whistled anthem to the storm
over wettened dirt in sodden grain fields.

A red fox feels through wet grass silently;
insects shake their soft-strong pedals, toning.
When the land is laid in, broken, bare,
for the seed to hit the fallow dirt we pray a good
end for its fertility.

The armies of suburban sprawl advance against
the troops of the ditch bank salient whose battle
lines are firm before the steel machines dig up
the boys of gaudy green whose waving locks live
on in memories.

Wetlands in the Mind

We sit beneath the sparkling sign of Buddy's
Pork Barbeque and lift a can of beer

in honor of the wetlands in our minds ...
over the sunset,
out of the gate,
burning ochre and crowned with agate
comes the night's pet;
a black cat
leaps through purplish mound to yellow mat
of smoking clouds ...
Around us blink the evening lights of neon
announcing fun,
movie stars and old age in the sun ...
while the egret,
creamy white,
stretches out dark legs,
circling round.
climbs from dregs
of water
high
to burning sky
and, silver in the light,
bathed and wet,
flies through the smoking clouds, until the black
cat scratches sun to make a kill
of Eden's glowing horizon ...

Then night birds
hunt for moths whose herds contest the sky
with neon pyres
lit to service my

Flight four-o-twelve
and beacons of infinite motels.

Voyager ...

Consider, confess a cosmic joke
in the subtileness of southern sea sun against the
corals made for other oceans
in service to quaint dinosaur folk,
not our Dionysus of mushroom smoke or our
sleek supertanker nations. Consider, uncover
the comedy in universal cannibalism of our sea;
its dainty,
embellished albatrosses spar with biting white
species of sharks, each preying in no-quarter war
on other creatures' hides they mark. Consider
how slowly the waves wear, tearing coral away
with the tides.
Noah's flood has not subsided; typhoons roil
two-thirds world's despair.

Environmental Aesthete

I want to grasp my fancy
by her chemically washed hands and pull the
lumpish woman back to a mystic vagrancy
beyond the isles and lands of Mab, to a grass
shack. Birds as well as planes have wings, but
skyscraper man wants props bought with
industrial gold and learns to despise the stings

of mosquitoes as malaprops
from a life covered with mold.
From my gardens stained with blight
I will try to harvest cankers
coated with a metaphor that's handy
substitute for Miller Lite
to replace the man-made, ranker weeds, whose
bitterness gags me.

October Evening

Above the still leaved trees a silver eye
floats on oceanic sky waiting for evening
breezes.

In the autumn twilight random footsteps softly
crunch the radiant, fallen leaves. Failing sunlight
glows on the lips of thieves who have stolen
their lunch from the forest's delights. Birds have
traveled beyond
the sparkling breast of an autumn pond.

In an old tavern under the tall trees a sad guitar
offers a song
below the dusty stairs whose creaky pleas
complain its boards have worked too long. As
the night falls a stranger
hears the music floating to his chamber

as sun fades to black velvet under moonlight
enveloping the sounds of night recalling hints of danger.
Above the still-leaved trees a silver eye
floats in star-studded sky waiting for morning breezes.

Seedtime

Red, yellow, turquoise colors catalog returning
swallows, gnats their emblem imprinted on the
mind as man and dog lazily chasing next year's
game and cim-lins ignore the hum of TV near
their rim of dream world as visions of birth
entice forth cornfield beans and fertilize them
though grouse and quail must bundle in the ice
as garden seed are bought at January's price.
Although seed catalogs encourage gems of
plants, winter reveries cannot last,
but it's a help to dream tomato stems to ease
discomfort at the winter's blast
and remind us of springs and harvests past.

Who Has Title?

A scenic view of meadow and cowbells includes
brindle leaning over bluebells
to green scum jelling a three-day mudhole, a
beauty unable to kindle joy

in the inspective gaze of the blind mole. The
grubby gentleman can but enjoy
worms and other delights too sweet to tell to
those who envy him in his dark hell. Eocene
vistas gave this bugbear
a rapid pulse beneath a coat of fur
which keeps him warm but hidden from air in
his dark lair away from the owner's barking,
nosing mutt—a notable cur
who seeks under grasses for old mole's fur.
Those ridges in the owner's lawn cause
heartburn and hunting at the hardware for a
mole trap to settle an ancient ownership scrap
that no old, enfranchised mole can discern.

Intersections on the Inland Waterway

Our minds travel ages in mysterious ways
creating images of the past to grace our present
so that our ancestors come alive in our days,
reincarnated in our suns' ascent.
My inland waterway meanders from coastal
waters to mountain streams around the world—
travels that span all continents and only loiter
when my dreams relive my joys and perils.

Fleeing westward, eyes on the smoky ridge
Appalachia raises beyond the coastal plain

a pilgrim seeks relief from city forms that bridge
bright streams until they groan and complain.
Mountains spur the mind of the dreamer ruing
Eden's fall to phallic embrace
yet raise ancestors roasting meatier portions
with hot embers to their taste.

Bodies bound, the leaping's of dreams address
fiery circles frying mammoth chops for hikers
yelling their hunger. Famished, tearing flesh,
erectus grabs and gnaws at the morsels.
Transported to the jungles of New Guinea
I join a jovial crew motoring down the Sepik
River to see what fearsome headhunters used to
be
as they enact old ways adorned in marsupial fur.

Next, Nantahalas shed their colored leaves into
the fogs of Cullowhee, Valley of Lilies, now
falling to chimneys and walls and eaves burned
in the fireplace of memories. Leaving the
mountain festival fall
I return to the swamp woods of my youth in
flatlands of Chesapeake where the katydids call
a welcome back to waterways of Powhatan.

There randy tunes of the fish crows and jaybirds
crack the stillness and blend with the hot hum of
mosquitoes and the whistle of the Southern

down the track as I meld with my forebears in
time's fast flow.

Ode to a Power Shortage

While the grunt of a dozer puts bread on our
tables
and sculpts a highwall
to the gods of progress,
the advocates of comfortable disease supply a
press release defying all our disbelief.

We sit and contemplate the valley hid with fill,
the wrecks of mountains, the wraith of dirt in
disarray dumped anywhere the Monied please
who borrow from the trees of yesterday.

What is Mt. Rushmore other than a wall, they
say,
of sculpted dirt and stone, a way of honoring our
past? So pay tribute to the present need whose
sores we justify to feed our deficits of energy.

Take It Off! Strip!

When I decry bulldozers tearing the land you
tell me, "Beauty is a biscuit!"
and threaten me with loss of livelihood and deep
breathing in my phone
at three a. m. In the daylight you demand

I see mountains as lumps of mud. You make pits
in serpentine circles where peaks stood as
continental backbone.

On every truck I read the boast, "I dig
Coal!" but where are the signs that add, "with
care"? Yeah, you've made thirty million in five
years of earthy rape and pillage:
so this black gold will be dug with your rigs
you'll turn mountains into empty air where a
man can't live and
high walls rear up to mark a dead village.

In Appalachia it's hard to argue jobs won't last as
long as scars upon the hills and the scars within
the soul that set our children's teeth on edge
when they look at mountains made into stobs or
leveled into the hollows as fill
to make a fast buck without a regret for
mechanical wreckage.

Silver Lawns

Some green vines turn brown at the first frost.
It silvers grass, astounds
vegetable stalks
until their sap is lost
as life defaults.
The Cumberlands burn

in October sun,
a brush painting fern
and green trees golden.
Potatoes newly dug
lie on the ground. We cough as we shiver and
shrug this beauty off.
Rumours spread the word that wooly worms are
furred so old man Mullins 'sees bad storms and
knows there'll be an early freeze and autumn
snow.
Leaves that were burnt red a week ago crackle
under the tread
of boots that go
to meet November wind. Hiking noisily home
tonight toward the autumn's end, crunching up
the hollow's light
before the hills turn white to cover tree leaves
shed
as snow softly embraces earth, we seek for new
birth on a squeaky bed.

Namibian Feasts: If You Want to Save SomeWildlife

Any African ecotourist
should have seen a zebra or a gnu,
a bat-eared fox or an oryx
and perhaps an elephant or two.

But some ecotourists are gourmets who prize
their wildlife cooked. Ranchers who make their
wildlife pay sell tourists steaks, after they've
looked.

Strange beasts abound at Roy's place where
Roy's wife cooks gourmet feasts for Namib
ecotourists' taste— exotic herbs and gamey
meats.

After you've birded Swakopmund and
pelicanned at Walvis Bay
you can drink good beer and eat a ton of
crocodile at Sussusvlei.

If you want to save world wildlife from people
whose habitat has beasts, then take up your fork
and knife. First look, and scope, enjoy, then eat.

Internal Blues

No Second Flights

My dove of youth that last year flew away did
not return this birthday.
This morning as I stand before the mirror
I see gray age my world abhors.
Tying my halter the old way
I see a rising sun glare at my back today.

My wrinkled face looks foul.
So many times we put on the wrong cowl for
defense against the looming storm yet can only
mourn its harm. I sent the wrong birds to scout.
My birds could only count the costs I had
incurred.

I should have sent a raven— they wear the
proper clothing,
can croak and soar with gutteral ease and roust
those fears that lurk dark seas. I shall pretend
my messengers were dark and hope to find
repose in my mind's ark.

Retrospection

I could not admire the passions I have had
passed down to me from some old stone age
man; although I could not judge them good or
bad, I know their anger has made me sad
and dragged me to that artless, unplanned but
frightened life which embodies glands that slew
old Adam. Doctors brought a cart to wheel me
off before I fell apart.
Age has brought calmer nerves and self-control,
so time has been a friend and enemy
whose patient work has left me quiet and whole
with pastel pleasures found in memories.

Satellite Map

This chart for my too unlit night
is not for Argus eyes imperative
upon the plains of platitudes;
this map I draw with seer-like sight beyond the
streams whose bulls must drive in forthright
cows' beatitudes— a plat to guide my frequent
flights avoiding bony, starving beeves, escaping
guard of Io eve, who may betray my latitudes.

A World of Afternoon

Artificers of imagined worlds are not confined
by stored heat—

we can create demesnes with concrete rules set
by imagination alone.

The mind's morning shadows drift away on
sliding cotton and red satin pleats flouncing red
through the day's doorway, until noon steps
through on hot feet from which white shoes
have been pulled to greet afternoon rainbows
whirling in the sun

like drunken tumblers that touch the hair of a
girl who pulls back strands to produce a curl of
lambent hair whose slow recoil's begun
to light flambeaux in the eyes of a hungry fox
who unfolds the colder husk of cloth stocks past
brown shoulders and pink nipples
to steal ivory grapes whose wine he tipples.

In the afternoon sun lizards
and foxes may share the heat in rocks; we jump
charge life with energetic shocks when mind-
created worlds collide.

After Parting

I think my heart a martyr or a saddened
bobolink with serenades of indigo, so many
yesterdays ago

my enemy cut us a pen apart with oceanic sink.
“I will shed tears, “ I said, “if you go because I am not free
to stow
away and follow
you to the cafes of Paris.”
That must have been ... how many years ago was it that I had to sew
my love together with the needled foe
of wait ‘til I return? An old poet missed his love so:
“I saw you last, I know, twenty or thirty years
before the clouds grumbled and the promised
flood tumbled down upon old Noah’s ears.”
Come back and see the mountainsides we climbed to watch the sun
burn life into the April myths homespun shaking their dainty latticed hides
at the disappearing snow on hillsides foretelling
that blooms upon the budding trees will unite
my love and me.

Ragged Tread

From my labored start faintly remembered
in kaleidoscopic moments of the motor’s whir—
become a part
of horizon’s fading remnant:
with studs to clutch

the mud grips of my mind engage to touch the
ice events of memory—I grind.

Intentions

Footsteps fell upon an empty path whose brown
leaves betrayed a blight and a halfway house of
harvest chaff where the crop ends in barn light,
unwinnowed sheaf for a staff.

Dirty feet wandered down a dusty path indented
with uncharted holes
even in dry autumn aftermath when the heat of
the forest doles last life careless of the hunter's
shaft.

I went to harvest delicious fruits
from the orchard ground where apples fell and
bent my ears to hear the owl's hoot as I
considered the sulphurous smell on my face and
hands and boots.

Cover-up

Sometimes my snow melts. My defenses fade on
mountains in my provinces.
As the ruler, I taste the guilt
for deaths that spring from indecision and
building walls of weak confusion.

In land of ruse where weak walls are built stands
the ruler's moldy house of unclear mind. No
children play except in fear
at shuttered windows and cracked sashes which
let in food for the owls.
Mice run under the moon's leer on old, wind-
scattered ashes
while new snows fall as the winds howl and
snow drifts gather in a white cowl.

Requiem for Nick

The tassel-crumpled corn suggests a plan, a
hoped-for harvest of sun-ripened grain, not
barren brush cut down on ditch banks before it
swells with fertility's rain.
Our hands outstretched, we mourn thwarted
design in small relief. Standing on harvest fields
with winter birds we sing decay's dark signs
whose shorter stalks imply our wraith-like deals.
For our farewells we shadows must be brief
for mourning those who haste away from us,
who, like green forests, succumb to a thief with
frosty hands. We must remember thus that
maple buds will redden limbs in light
of spring when love and lilies flash their white.

Seekers

Climbing the Matterhorn in the morning dawn
means only that we'll wish
by evening that the Hindu Kush had been the
object of our scorn.

Heat Wave Past ...

We fell in love with an ancient notion of
chivalry romancing vows exchanged beneath an
arbor greened by emotion— lovers' flowery
bowers trouveres arranged with centuries of
songs regaling moons. We woke to find us
strangers who too soon found out, flowers
withered, lovers weep vegetable tears for
bouquets in June
as warblers sing. We remembered out of tune
the twilight songs begun with lovers' sleep: we
sit like statues in an antique shop whose disdain
seems apt to signal complete the wreckage of
our vows we made to stop the living deaths of
lovers lacking heat.

Winter Mulch

Snow falls tonight
and I am sad for loss of autumn leaves.
Remember how we sat
and watched leaves fall in clear light?
We were at peace

as the gold and red relief erased the dark mat
with painted leaf.
I wish that snowflakes
brought quiet without heartache.

Whispers

When I was fifteen
We brought maples and oaks
From the ditch bank and planted our yard
With these and some mail-order trees,
Pecans and peaches and pears green
To the gaze and shading the folks
Throughout the years that they stood guard
And cradled a cool breeze.

Voices murmur at me
From the rooms my hands have emptied To fill a
rented moving truck
For hauling off the furnishings of their lives,
And mine, across the hills and away from the sea
In a nervous excitement of a free
Flight from the thought of being struck
When the mockingbird dives.

Growth

For long, long years I rumbled, ranted and raved
incessantly about life's shallow worth;

my mad motors grumbled, and axes were
ground by me, simply to satisfy my dearth;

and then, how odd, humbled;
I realized the soul's great majesty, increased my
girth.

The End of Youth

In dreams I traveled far around the world with
Sinbad and put aground
on lands that had
not once been bound
by human minds, I thought, since beautiful
Scheherazade breathed her storied incense
about the Caliph's harsh charade.

Then I journeyed past tropical isles and slipped
by horizons in a fast and white-rigged ship that
never returned
to its brilliant slip
after I spurned
the sails that wafted me where
I floated on breezes of purple air

until three wrathful monkeys summoned
dragons and grinned a wry grin as firedrakes
burned my skies despite my naive pleas.

Debriefing

Conquer, will we ever? Well I doubt it when a
primate urge reigns in my head and tingles all
the nerve-ends that I own with cries to seek that
momentary high adrenalined with heat to make
us writhe in a damp bed where we awake the
dead.

Nerve ends frozen, what's the gain to have them
rendered calm through chilly subterfuge, the
ancient thrill electric over now?
Batteries of DNA always run down,
but human hearts demand a jumper start and
cannot live for long without some heat.

Philemon to Baucis

We have spent long years together in good times
and foul weather.
Our love is not a storybook romance nor the
heat inside the groin although you know you stir
me there, yet not with a come-hither glance or
memory of the bright dawns before we settled
our affair.
How can an ardent lover say, "You make me
comfortable and tolerate my follies." These
words do not display the bellowing rut of a bull
nor kisses by magnolia trees,
but you and I live every day at ease.

Bus Trip

Around a bend a winding of horn, as my love in
green goes riding, her beauty unseen but gliding
—a waif greeting the dawn.
Inside the station a girl with Chinese eyes sips
her green tea whose color
held in two hands implies an attempt to do
honor to a most ancient Ming, but the old
Emperors Ching didn't chew tomato sandwiches
away
nor get asked what they would have today by a
short- order Mother Hubbard twin who is very
helpful but hardly Confucian. She's extremely
cheery,
"Don't miss your bus, Dearie.
Don't despair. You're going somewhere." We're
throwing off old traces and really going places.
Good fortune cookies await us there. Good-bye,
good- bye, my friends, soon our journey ends,
but my love in green will go riding on, gliding
into the dawn.

Command Performance

Seize the unshaped eager nights for graces and
care that a too-swift clock rushes us untaught to
command our naked feet
and thoughts that prompt our too-quick races
and a sweat on our brows that brushes

off silky clouds surrounding our retreat with
thoughts to give our dappled traces a bright
dawn with sated satyrs' horn
and transfixes our hearts with nagging fears of
losing scenes that touch our eyes and ears with
an eager mouth whose kisses seem born in lilac
odors tasting of sweet tears— until our batteries
revive desire
as artists of life find much love's required.

Afternoon Mail

Yearning for Ponce de Leon's fountain
of youth in moments of dark thoughts that stain
my mind after my latest mailbox trip,
I ponder life's recent rejection slip. We grant the
very old and very young the right to vent anger
that touches hearts and spills the dark distress
that has stung their minds, but mature age craves
silent arts. In black moments of self-pitying care
I opt for dumb reverie of despair.

Fire Escape

Hunters on the veldt in the Pleistocene— a
group of clever, biped animals
cringe and snarl at night their hate of unseen
fears and snatch embers to brandish fireballs.
Habilis to Homo sapiens ran
when fiery hands threw out flame brands.

Today, snarling in kraals, modern sun-hued
beasts with metallic claws sport being man
using high tech to torch savannah lands with
powder- dark hands whose fire's released when
angry hands throw out firebombs. Homo sapiens
to terrorist succumbs
as dark genes reassert ancient demands and new
horrors stalk in modern lands.

The Game Is Fixed

Here we must sit, the dealers and the dealt. Poor
poker players have no place to go
and dealers show no love for those who've felt
they could bet weak whores against a foe
who holds a full house hand and bluffs as well,
but we players cannot leave this game and go to
other tables. Our strength cannot impel
a change of games. We play a harsh high-low.

My First Trip to Chicago. 1956

In Chicago I went on a visit to a very religious
family keen
to burn out blacks who had bought a lot and
built a house down their street. Their eyes
expected my eyes complicit atavism to echo
what I had seen

when a young man's rage fueled hatred's rot: my
conscience dredged up a dark conceit. Growing
up in Virginia as a boy
who wanted his buddies to accept him I acted
out sick body's hatred
of niggahs with ritual.
Driving down the highway with angry joy of
malt liquor in our hands and a grim curse on our
lips, we sought victims to shred our tender,
civilized shawl.
Laughter erupted in our car as black bodies
jumped from the edge of the road to escape the
rush of our oncoming car lunging at
defenselessness.
As we swerved to avoid the ditch and crack up,
we established ourselves in the code as we
hurled our empty cans as far as we could in our
excess
of cheerfulness. We cheered when we scored a
hit on the figures crouching in the drainage ditch
like a frenzied crowd cheering the home team's
annihilation of their foes.
No matter that the morning after fit my
conscience ill. The emotional pitch achieved by
unleashing our anxious dreams nourished
diseased egos.

After reading Faulkner, I thought men's doubts
had conjured up the hate that threw the cans and

curses. I thought to blame grandfather, or at
least the Klu Klux Klan.
Then I took my trip to Chicago's shout-filled
streets and watched the wary Africans while
they eyed me sidling down their corridor of
concrete jungle land.

Almost alone in a swarm of dark faces
I sensed a hatred akin to what spurred my arm
those nights along the ancient southern way. I
saw myself reflected
in their eyes. I had disowned their race
as not akin to me. The wind from the storm that
shook me blew a black man's hat my way as
forceful gusts directed
a deed of reparation for old guilt.

Stooping down I picked up the brown fedora,
brushed out a bruise, and extended the hat to a
bewildered man, adjusting the blade of his fear
with a tilt; he stood awhile in an amazed aurora
before extending a hand to take the hat and
absolve my lack of tan.

Thermostat Control

A mystic madman stands in the half-light at
open doors and listens to the dark bird who
sings to announce his evening flight; the listener

hears as a sightless person stirred to cast off the
iron mask whose prison covers with rusty wrap
the mental jumps he does not trust because his
indecision negates faith in his crimson heat
pump.
The angelus of the hermit thrush in his ears
signals his need to retreat
to a place where the sounds of day are hushed
and the sensuous fare of Phaedria's feast does
not lead to the
dirty morning daze
for those who lurch within her stupored maze.
Her minions gasp for air like fish upon land.
Burning in the sun the bloating pygmies cavort
with glee upon her floating island that moves
aimlessly to and fro too free, from gloom to
glow—itinerary they feel will avoid all the rocky,
rougher roads
and help to ease their fears with prayer wheels
to provide a fleshy salvation mode:
"Oh for a cup of gladness and delight," implore
those seeking lotus without life. To the mystic in
his innermost flights comes a vision of blood
beneath a bier where a butchered bull must feel
knife's bite to make red flow on the proselyte's
fears.

The pilgrim's unbroached pump with valves
working lets him see the flight of birds without
fear; now his mental wheels are interlocking
and his higher pressure lets him play the seer.
He can climb to the city on the hill
or take the way of meditation meant for those
who would pure thought distil under a Bo tree of
enlightenment.
Those who repair the interlocking wheels defeat
Phaedria's power to deceive
those whose crimson pulsating machines feel the
strength of their red heat pump to achieve a
victory for soul bird's evening show.
That stirs strong flow in the pilgrim's dynamo.

Comic Blues

Cheers!

Too grand a view of courage, kid, will mar your
chances for success. Where can a fellow find an
Id these days with nothing to confess?

You say you will face bravely met, the world, yet
seek a trace of mirth. Let us then, you and me,
go wet
our stomachs down and seek new birth.

In Venus' bar no doubt will be
a girl to give us strength to chase our cares into a
Daiquiri.
Let us curse fate bravely, but with grace.

Cakes and Ale

Malvolio, you've had it. Your time has fled by
clock and fire and water, wind, and see
how little dint you made in immorality by
washing mud from social scenes and
whimpering at the foaming head

sucked off the beer and making public preen to
gain a second's immortality
while lovers laugh and lip upon the green
and pay no heed to those who preach obscene.

A Consideration

The Legalists told Mencius that man is fuss and
lust; he should not seek
for men both good and sleek.
Mencius pondered about
it. He answered in a polite shout:
man is mostly good!
The sage has not been understood.

Street Scene

There walks a man ruing late down the street
tandem with mate, with sighs and grimaces
marching by his magistrate.
He tends the tares he sowed early by accepted
code;
he now is firmly led to places where formerly he
strode.

He slyly watches calves career eliciting his
secret leer— subversive in his traces,
responds submissively, "Yes, dear."

Vamp

There goes a pixie prancing dressed in red,
fitted for summer dancing on green beds.
She is the glow of evening, its soft light,
meeting the dark with scheming looking to the
night. Lithe dance and whispered chants make
sweet moments while revel girl plants thoughts
in forment—. Whacked hair in boyish cut,
laughing leers pert
upon a row of gleaming teeth, portrait of a flirt.

Clancy to the Poet

Don't hand me that guff about artist stuff, just
pay your bill and be decent enough. That's all I
ask of any man: eat well, pay reg'lar, be part of
the clan.
You have the God-given right to overstuff.
Disregard the flimflams of fancy.
Its freedom is risky, it's too damn chancy. Why
should you argue the dictates of pooh-poohing
critical pates when you can dine out with Mrs.
Clancy? Don't starve in a jail, or up in a garret;
art is not food or a cigarette. Why dally around
with a Muse
when you can have any girl you choose, and
gallons of beer and cellars of claret?

Snake-eyes

A philosophy of carpe diem appealed to Abou-
hem; one might say his whim
was the stem of Abou-hem's desire.
So he touched his lyre,
looked forward every day to dine and sip good
wine, until one unfortunate night,
pushed over a precipice while throwing dice the
hedonist was caught in a trice. Aware of his
plight,
he began muttering prayers; he repeated them
thrice
as the way to Paradise, but the gist of his impasse
and his unlucky cast
forced him down to devilish affairs.

Adamite Orchardists

He hungered for my apple trees because his
fruits weren't good enough, but instead of
planting other trees
he cut my orchard down to the duff. His apples
win all the prizes now; he foresees blue ribbons
at State Fair and has ordered a suit for his bow.
He will curse those trees I picked bare.

Indigestion

Metallic cones give off peals inviting hollow
dreams: our Gargantua's plight comes from guts

of steel outhelching smoke and screams to
heckle day and night.
It would be fit fuel to inveigh greatly offended
laughter from old master Rabelais, whose gross
methane after dinner came from healthy farts,
not from mechanical arts.

Politically Incorrect Advice

In arguments with wives about the shop-ping
men should do, a clever ploy might
be to cite a bit of ancient history:
in Athens women worked indoors, adopting
tasks set forth by Homer as the right of goddess,
wife, and daughter; slavery must fetch the water
jugs; discreetly
they flirted and gossiped at fountain sites,
but matrons cared for children, nursed the sick
and sewed and cooked; for Platea's siege the
fighting men were left behind women to sop
the soldiers' hunger. Surely manly tricks can win
our sexual battles if we're slick.
If trained, our wives might even shop for mops.

A Fact of Life

One sunny green-shod day in a very natural way
I climbed out into the world, or you might say
fate hurled

me past life's gate across a threshold from warm-
ness out to cold,
I'm told, for I must admit I think I came a bit
unwillingly from my mother's fold.
We passed an hour or two with song before I
stood upon my feet. I could
not wait for long before I thought me strong
enough to face harsh life. Alas, though Mother
paid my fee,
I found the doctor's knife had never cut me free.

Busy Old Fool and Friend

Holding his two heads between his hands
gingerly pleading a hedonist's case,
he addressed his unwelcome visitor, "You've
brought a beautiful day, my man, but why don't
you go away. It's a waste. I'll stagger back to bed,
inquisitor."
To his grief, that morning his bosom friend had
climbed up fast and full of fun to grin on
bloodshot eyes, on yawning, cursing man who
acted out his anger unrehearsed. Sleepy, shaking
his fist with bleak chagrin he told his buddy, "I
don't need a tan." Eyeing the bottle on his desk,
he cursed his happy friend. Barely able to thin
the gray confusion in his throbbing head, he
addressed his sun, "O jinn of the gin, I am
inclined to think I'm almost dead. After long

nights with Gilby's and a whore (here he was
forced to blink) you are a bore. You, bragging,
bumptious sun, are no fun. Do not force yourself
on my attention." The hotshot denied the plea to
vacate.
In his meddling style, he heated away in
disregard of his bosom buddy's pate.
Unhindered by clouds, he blazed out all day.

A Flamboyant's Birthday

For a year Ralph Teutsch has burned among us.
His fiery zeal has seared the sullen flesh of many
a wayward youth in calculus.

Now has his flame burned two and twenty years
toward his last problem in the finite math, and
his presence warms us as it sears.

As geometric wheels turn on our wires and our
machines must calculate his day, we thank him
his bright fuel to our fires.

Eddie Guest, I Know You

You're a poet singing lasses,
sad souls, and sentimental asses.
You've gnawed the bone of sentiment
and whined or wagged your way to print—
would build a house beside a road

and be a friend to man, a mode
of life that moves your readers' hearts, for they
adore your canine arts. Their handkerchiefs
always at hand to wipe the tear you make to
stand
on grim cheeks, they find your aphorisms turn
too blank glass to prisms
that change their earth from dross to gold, I'm
told, that will not tarnish nor grow old. You coat
old truths with stickiness; you're a mutt with
craftiness.

You Can't Hike in Kruger, and the Zulu Are on Strike

The Kruger warden carried on though the Zulu
were on strike.
All night the Zulu drums and Zebu horns argued
Zulu wages should be hiked.

The warden sighed...
"Tsk, tsk!" the warden's lady cried,
"Here come the ecotourists. They can't hike and
the Zulu are on strike.
What shall we do?"
"We'll roll out a van or two
and take them to the nearest hide, let them see a
zebra, nyala, or gnu, or perhaps a lion pride."

"Oh no, dear, haven't you heard? These are
Americans hot after birds. They beat the bush in
their own vans, but they must eat. How can we
feed this herd with the Zulu striking, every
man?"

They met us sadly, wringing hands.
The warden warned, "You can't hike in Kruger
and our food supplies are slender since the Zulu
are on strike, and their drums don't let you sleep
at night."

For us ecotourists things seemed rather grim.
We could not hike in Kruger
and the food seemed mighty meager. We feared
we must pack it in,
but dauntless Ian Sinclair led us. He asked for
gnu and kudu steaks. While we birded aboard
our bus, the kudu marinated
as we counted birds and debated how cold beers
ease stomach aches.

At night the cold beer flowed while steaks
sizzled on the grills
and appetites began to grow—and grow. Result—
a gamey gourmet thrill.

So, in Kruger where you cannot hike, do not let
yourself despair if the Zulu are on strike.

Just ask to eat some kudu fare.

Adaptation

When boys are small, they are happily inclined,
yet the elders feel that all
should toil
manfully and grind
approval's seal.
So boys take castor oil
and learn to make
piled mountains out of mole hills
and take, for victory's sake, a bitter pill.

Ben Ezra's Fraud

I am growing grayer Robert Browning, and new
medical technology does not help me accept my
senses fading away like old soldiers. Your
promise was
the best was yet to be. The sounds, the tastes,
the smells, the sights have all grown less acute. I
feel a pinch of flab about my waist, see no
reports that I am more astute than I was when
my hair was thick and black. I must confess I still
enjoy my life
even though I fear sudden heart attacks and
wonder how to satisfy my wife despite deep
new wrinkles and little hair, arsenal of pills and
calorie care.

Still, our age gives great boon—we love and live,
and I am loath for the alternative.

ABOUT THE AUTHOR

Peake published early poems in Impetus and in The Georgia Review. Collections of his poetry include Wings Across ..., (Vision Press, 1992), Birds and Other Beasts (Lettra Press LLC 2020), and Earth and Stars (Lettra Press LLC 2020), among others. Recent poems have appeared in Avocet, Boundless 2014, Enigmatist, Red River Review, Shine Journal, The Road Not Taken, and elsewhere. A life-long naturalist, a father, and grandfather, he has published 5 novels and is also out in the market: Jaykyll's Joust, Moon's BLACK GOLD, Beauty'S No Biscuit, Love and Death on Safari, and Rare Bird Alert. All novels got outstanding reviews from professional book reviewers.

www.ingramcontent.com/pod-product-compliance
Lightning Source LLC
LaVergne TN
LVHW011933070526
838202LV00054B/4615
* 9 7 8 1 9 5 8 5 5 4 3 2 6 *